Praise for *The Zigzag Principle*

"Entrepreneurs, you need *not* fear failure anymore! With *The Zigzag Principle* in hand, you will have all the tools you need to increase your probability of success the instant you apply the concepts in this book."

—*Rick Sapio, founder and CEO of Mutual Capital Alliance, Inc.*

"*The Zigzag Principle* isn't feel-good fluff—it is a logical and practical formula that you can put your hands on, and it *will* increase the rate of success of any business you apply it to."

—*Moe Abdou, principal and founder, 33 Voices*

"*The Zigzag Principle* is more powerful than the "release and iterate" mentality that is so prevalent today. I have adjusted my planning to incorporate this principle in our product launches. Properly executed, *The Zigzag Principle* will keep folks like me out of financial hot water."

—*David McInnis, founder of PRWeb.com; founder and CEO of Cranberry LLC, Venture Partners*

"Most entrepreneurs find it complicated and difficult to build their businesses. Rich has done a masterful job with *The Zigzag Principle* to make complex things simple and difficult things easy—and it works! It will help you get where you want to be with more confidence and certainty."

—*Murray Smith*, New York Times *bestselling author of* The Answer; *CEO of MainStreetMentor.com*

"Whether you are a parent, an entrepreneur, a factory worker, or a middle manager, *The Zigzag Principle* will provide you with a framework and a formula that will empower you to make changes in your world you had never felt were possible."

—*Joseph Grenny,* New York Times *bestselling coauthor of*
Influencer: The Power to Change Anything

"*The Zigzag Principle* delivers *the epiphany of the decade* for business owners. These strategies are nonintuitive, but proven to be solid and dependable, which is why this is such an important work. Not only will you profit faster than you thought possible, you'll also enjoy greater balance and fulfillment in the process."

—*Leslie Householder, award-winning bestselling author of*
The Jackrabbit Factor: Portal to Genius

"I don't believe entrepreneurship is something you can truly learn from a book. Everyone has to make their own mistakes. Nevertheless, if you've already made some mistakes, then you'll find *The Zigzag Principle* to be a no b.s. guide to starting, nurturing, and succeeding at entrepreneurship."

—*Jeffrey Eisenberg,* New York Times *and*
Wall Street Journal *bestselling author of*
Call to Action *and* Waiting for Your Cat to Bark?

The Zigzag Principle

The Goal-Setting Strategy That Will Revolutionize Your Business and Your Life

RICH CHRISTIANSEN

New York   Chicago   San Francisco   Lisbon   London
Madrid   Mexico City   Milan   New Delhi
San Juan   Seoul   Singapore
Sydney   Toronto

1 2 3 4 5 6 7 8 9 10   DOC/DOC   1 6 5 4 3 2 1

ISBN 978-0-07-177458-1
MHID 0-07-177458-0

e-ISBN 978-0-07-177527-4
e-MHID 0-07-177527-7

McGraw-Hill books are available at special quantity discounts to use as premiums and sales promotions or for use in corporate training programs. To contact a representative, please e-mail us at bulksales@mcgraw-hill .com.

This book is printed on acid-free paper.

Contents

Acknowledgments

I grew up in a family of four boys. I have five sons. There have only been two women in my life, both angels. My beautiful wife is not only my inspiration but she is my source of strength and resolve. She was vital in all ways in my writing this book, including the composition of much of the text. My mother died when she was still young, but the lessons that she taught me still burn strong.

I thank Jim Bell for editing the book and the masterful way that he is able to weave and blend my stories and Wayne Pullman for his wonderful graphics. Also intimately involved in the efforts of this book were Curtis Blair, my partner and general manager of Froghair; Garrett Gunderson, who twisted my arm into doing this; and Michael Drew, my agent. Bill Erb is a confidant who helped me keep my head on straight and convinced me to strap on a jet pack to push forward on this book.

I also wish to thank my sons and their friends, who have spent countless hours listening to me lecture to them on the Zigzag Principle.

Deliberate Detours

Not long ago, I took my 14-year-old son skiing for only his third time. In getting off the lift, we accidentally took a wrong turn and ended up with nowhere to go but down a ridiculously steep, black diamond run. As we stood at the top of this cliff, this inexperienced skier looked down in sheer horror and exclaimed: "I am going to die!"

In an attempt to calm his understandable fears, I explained that he didn't need to head straight down the mountainside, that even an expert skier would survey the drop we stood at the top of and decide to zigzag down the steep slope. I instructed him not to look at the bottom of the run, but to focus on skiing to a point across the hill and, once there, to turn and ski back across the slope to another preselected point.

As a concerned father, I knew my son's chances of getting to the bottom without breaking his leg or neck were far greater with this approach than if he had just barreled straight down the mountain. No question, it took us a while to make our way down, but as he stood at the bottom of the run and looked back up to where he had started, he realized the full import of what he had accomplished—and the lesson he had learned.

When I graduated some 20 years ago with my MBA, my mindset was the exact opposite of what I had shared with my son. I was certain I could excel in business by sheer force and determination. I truly believed that my success would come by setting my sights on a goal and then going straight for it. With that as my strategy, I plowed toward my goals no matter what was in my way. In fact, I plowed through things that had no business being plowed through.

I clearly remember the person who first called me on my tendency. His name was Vish. Vish was always railing on me. He was a brutal boss, and he took every occasion to tell me what I was doing was wrong. He could drive me, a grown businessman, to tears.

One day, Vish came into my office and said, "Rich, let me show you what your problem is!" (This was how many of my conversations with Vish started, but this time our exchange was eye opening.) He walked over to my door and deliberately locked and then unlocked it. When it was unlocked, he swung it open and said, "This is a door that actually opens. You do not always have to try to bust the door down. All you have to do is unlock it and then turn the doorknob."

As I thought about what he had said, I realized how many times I had chosen not to use the doorknob in my career. I had just tried to plow through the door—locked or unlocked. In so doing, I was living contrary to a law of nature. Nature does not intend for me to walk through closed doors anymore than it expects my son to point his skis straight downhill and go.

While working in corporate America after graduating from business school, I experienced some significant successes (Vish's periodic rants notwithstanding). And, since striking out on my own, I have founded or cofounded 32 businesses. Of these ventures, 11 were ugly failures, 8 have enjoyed moderate success, 2 are in progress, and 11 have become multimillion-dollar wins. Even after Vish's object lesson, it took me a long time to be willing to pause at the bottom of the mountain, look back up to the top, and see the epiphany that had been eluding me. When I was finally willing to take the time to look back, I saw that my most significant accomplishments—whether working for someone or for myself—

did not come when I charged directly toward my goal. Rather, they came when I zigged and zagged my way to success.

I realized that the diversions and detours I had often found so frustrating had actually created more stable and solid businesses. On the other hand—and without exception—each time I had raced directly at a target with high velocity, I had failed.

This realization came to me several years ago as a business partner, Ron Porter, and I were writing a book titled *Bootstrap Business: A Step-by-Step Business Survival Guide.* As we wrote this book, we decided to start a business in order to test, prove, and illustrate for our readers the principles we were writing about. As I had done with several other successful startups, we each anted up $2,500 for a staggering total of $5,000 in startup capital. That was it. We could have brought more money to the table, but we were out to prove that we could bootstrap a business and turn it into at least a million-dollar asset.

With no idea of what this business was going to be, but with our working capital in place, the first thing that we did was to assess our resources. We had $5,000 in cash, several contacts in New York, some solid business and technology experience, and combined expertise in web development. We then ran what is called the "Porter Model" on various possibilities we had identified, ultimately deciding to create an online entrepreneurs' social network.

We started down our chosen path by developing and then revising the website, www.bootstrapbusiness.org. But we very quickly realized that it would take a lot more money than $5,000 to reach our goal. So we immediately detoured and accepted some search engine optimization (SEO) consulting engagements with several large East Coast corporations. Why? We had to chase cash.

As soon as we were turning a profit with our consulting, we veered in another direction by hiring software engineers to do contract labor for several of our new clients. In doing so, we were adding resources to our business. And, serendipitously, we now had at our disposal developers who could work on our original website as well.

We then made another change in our course and started doing web link building. This is how we were able to start scaling our business as we created several supportive viral websites.

Before we went to press with *Bootstrap Business*, we were able to claim victory with the company we named CastleWave. This little test case we had started with $5,000 cash ended up being profitable every single month. It grew to become a multi-million dollar business, it won many awards in the community, and we sold it to a publicly traded company. Midway through the development of CastleWave, Ron and I were sitting at our whiteboard, plotting the paths we were taking toward our target. Originally, in keeping with the mindset I came out of business school with, we had outlined our starting point and our end goal. It was essentially a straight line. Somewhere along that line, however, we realized we needed a million to a million and a half dollars to hit our goal. Seeing that our original course was just not possible, we started drawing a sequential series of steps that needed to occur.

As we stepped back, we realized there was a big "Z" on the board. More specifically, there were three distinct targets we needed to hit in order to meet our first series of goals. First, we had to get to cash. Second, we had to add resources. And, third, we needed to scale our business. Each of these steps required an entirely different mindset from the one before. Even after having been subjected to Vish's scolding years before, this was my moment of full clarity as I realized that—just like skiing down a ski slope—getting to our goals requires a deliberate set of zigzags. This was the moment when the Zigzag Principle was formally defined.

Since this realization, it has been interesting for me to see that before I defined the steps of the Zigzag Principle, my business model was that I would succeed one out of three times. In fact, I would create three businesses, consciously telling myself, "Okay, of these three, one is going to fail, one is going to be mediocre, and one is going to turn into a multi-million dollar business." I figured I was batting about .333 with a series of strikeouts, easily caught pop-ups to left field, and hits that scored. Frankly, I was feeling pretty good about my average. But, in looking back, I've realized I was zigzagging, just without any real structure or discipline. Ever since my moment of clarity, I have been consciously applying the formal structure of the Zigzag Principle, and my success rate has dramatically increased. My partners and I have now had four out of five successes—an average I'll take any day.

As I've considered this revelation, I've come to realize that the Zigzag Principle has its roots in the laws of nature, with evidences everywhere we look. Rivers don't flow in a straight line from mountain springs to the ocean. They twist and turn as they adapt to the obstacles that impede their flow. Mountain peaks are formed by the violent acts of nature, which leave no straight shots to the top. So much of the beauty we see in nature is the result of its forces carving out paths that must wend their way around never-ending obstacles.

My family and I are avid hikers and love to climb mountains. We've scaled summits in the Rocky Mountains and in the Himalayas. In all our years of climbing, we've never been able to actually climb straight toward the peak. Instead, just as my son learned as he skied down the mountain, we've had to hike the switchbacks in order to reach the top of the mountain. In the process, we have found ourselves going around large canyons and cliffs, often hiking in directions opposite to the summit.

We have also found, while hiking in the Himalayas, that it is important not to gain too much altitude too quickly. Those who do, often succumb to high-altitude sickness and even death. Although it seems counterintuitive, much of the time, you actually have to lose altitude and hike away from your goal in order to stay healthy, build strength, and gain the altitude needed to get to your destination. As I have become more seasoned in both business and life, the lessons of the Zigzag Principle have finally begun to sink in. Life and business are complex and often messy, and there are always going to be bumps, dips, twists, turns, and detours along the routes we choose to pursue. It is unrealistic to think you can just charge directly at a goal without injuring yourself or others. Adjustments and course directions are always required.

I have an associate who has been extremely successful at racing directly toward his financial goals. He is charismatic, focused, business savvy, and driven. At the point we became acquainted, this man was well respected, a pleasure to be around, and an integral part of the community. Soon after, though, he became obsessed with becoming wealthy. In fact, he openly proclaimed that he would achieve his financial goal at any cost. In his pursuit to do so, there were marked changes in his demeanor and in his approach to life.

Within five years he had accomplished his goal of becoming the wealthiest individual in the community. But at what cost? His relationships with his spouse, his children, and his trusted associates were obliterated. He lost the love and respect of nearly everyone around him. Now, when his name is spoken in public, people recoil. Why? Because he ran roughshod over anyone and anything that attempted to divert him from his goal. Was his financial success worth barreling down the mountain with wild abandon? No! The end victory proved hollow and meaningless as he left behind the important things of life that he could and should have enjoyed. I would contend that he could have been successful in all aspects of his life had he traversed his way down the mountain instead.

The more effective and rewarding way of achieving long-term goals is to zigzag toward them. It is hard work in both hiking and in business, but the vistas and rewards are, without question, worth it.

COMPONENTS OF THE ZIGZAG PRINCIPLE

Before you can begin to zig and zag, there are certain foundational elements that you must build upon in order to succeed, as well as some critical tools you will need. This book is organized around the following tried-and-true principles that will help you make your way to the top of any peak you decide to summit.

1. Assessing resources
2. Identifying your beacon in the fog
3. Creating catalyzing statements
4. Driving to profitability
5. Defining processes and adding resources
6. Scaling your business
7. Staying within your guardrails
8. Developing reward systems

Chapters 1 through 3 provide your foundation, which I like to compare to a road trip. Think of the resources as your vehicle. It may be an old clunker that, on a good day, may get you across town. It may be a jacked-up, high-powered four-wheel drive that knows no fear. Or it may be a vintage

Mercedes that you'll only drive when there is not a cloud on the horizon. Think of the beacon in the fog as your destination. When you jump in your car in New York City and decide you're heading to San Francisco, there's no way you can see the Golden Gate Bridge. But you know it's there, and, if you're smart, you've mapped out a route that will take you there. Think of catalyzing statements as the fuel that will get you to your goal. Once you get the foundation for your business in place, then you can begin to zig and zag. The Zigzag Principle for growing your business follows a specific pattern:

⇨ Zig number 1: Always Get to Cash (Chapter 4)

⇨ Zag number 2: Adding Resources (Chapter 5)

⇨ Zig number 3: Scaling the Business (Chapter 6)

In Chapter 7, we'll discuss how important it is to establish your own personal guardrails so you don't find yourself driving off a cliff as you fly down the road. I'll share mine, and I'll encourage you to find yours.

Chapter 8 introduces the concept of reward systems. Zigzagging is hard work. And now and then you need to pause and reward yourself, your associates, and those family members and friends who are supporting you.

This book is a step-by-step tactical book. It is not a theory or a vague concept. You will get practical application tips you can use to succeed, not just in business but also in life. In addition, you will be provided with a suite of resources and tools that you can use online and offline to assist and use in your progression. To find these tools go to www.zigzag principle.com.

In my years in business—whether working for someone or pursuing my own dreams—I have had several multi-million dollar failures, in addition to several multi-million dollar successes. Many of the failures were of my own doing; and, thankfully, enough of them were not. I can honestly say that, in most instances, I failed because I tried to go straight for my goal and then ran out of gas before I hit profitability. The Zigzag Principle is not easy. It requires discipline, hard work, tenacity, and focus. It is not a lazy man's game. And it is what will help you achieve the successes you seek.

ONE

Assessing Resources— What's in Your Pocket?

A fter I wrote my first book, *Bootstrap Business,* which told the story of how my partner, Ron Porter, and I took $5,000 and within one year grew it into a $1.2 million business, I had the opportunity to be interviewed by Garrett Gunderson

13

for a national radio show. Garrett is the author of the *New York Times* bestseller, *Killing Sacred Cows,* and he started the interview by asking, "Rich, tell me about how you started this last business." I said, "Oh, I took $5,000 and . . ." Garrett interrupted me midsentence and said, "No! No you didn't."

I was kind of stunned and tried to explain, "Well, yes, I actually *did* start it with $5,000." He corrected me again, "No you didn't." And I retorted, "Yes, I did!"

After what I initially thought was a rather awkward beginning, Garrett went on to explain that the $5,000 my partner and I put up was the smallest part of the equation. In fact, in his words, the money was really meaningless. And in making that point, Garrett was teaching an invaluable lesson.

Most people assume we need to have money to succeed in business and to reach our goals in life. If we want to start a business, the reasoning goes, we first need capital. If we're given a major project at work, we immediately want to know what our budget is. If we want to take our family on a much-needed vacation, the first thing we do is check the balance of our bank account (or, if we really enjoy paying interest, our credit cards). That view develops a straight-line mentality as we undertake whatever we have set our sights on—whether it's a house, a business, a contribution to our team at work, a strong marriage and a stable family . . . you name it. But if all you think in terms of is how much money you need to achieve your goals, you're missing the fact that success is actually the result of identifying and maximizing a couple of foundational resources that have nothing to do with our traditional view of "capital" and have everything to do with zigzagging toward our intended outcome.

The point Garrett was making was that Ron and I succeeded because of what he calls "The Value Equation," which is that *mental capital* (meaning our knowledge, skills, talents, and passions) plus our *relationship capital* (meaning the quality of our relationships with a broad pool of friends and associates) will equal *financial capital*.

MENTAL CAPITAL   **RELATIONSHIP CAPITAL**   **FINANCIAL CAPITAL**

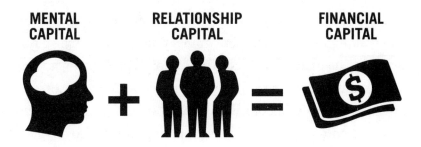

Yes, at some point money is often needed if we are to reach our goals. But that form of capital will grow out of the knowledge and the relationships we have, and the pace at which it grows will be influenced in large measure by our passion. If you need proof of this point, consider this extremely condensed list of transformative businesses that got their start in a college dorm room or garage: Apple, Facebook, Microsoft, Hewlett-Packard, and Google. And while the founders of each of these companies are now household names worth billions, they all began with little more than their smarts and their passion to achieve their goals, combined with their networks of friends.

This view of capital is very different from how most of us think about resources, and most people get the equation backwards. We think, "If only I had some money, I could reach my goals or realize my dreams." Money cannot build intelligence, relationships, or passion. But intelligence, relationships, and passion can always yield money. Coming to this view, though, may require you to adjust your thinking.

A few years after I graduated from college with a degree in electronic engineering, I enrolled in an executive MBA program while working for Novell, then the pioneer in computer networking (and yet another company founded by four guys with little capital, a bright idea, and a lot of passion—who are now multimillionaires). The vice president in charge of the division where I worked was Dave Owens. As I neared the completion of my MBA, I was preparing to move to another division in the company. Before I made the move, Dave called me into his office and asked me a simple question: "Rich, who do you work for?" The answer seemed obvious, and I told him I worked for him. His response was "Wrong!" and that was the end of that meeting.

A week later he called me back in and again asked me, "Rich, who do you work for?" Well, I had been thinking about his question, and this time I confidently told him, "Novell!" Again, he told me I was wrong. A week or so later, his administrative assistant made yet another appointment. I rather timidly went into his office, only to be asked the same question for the third time. But this time when he asked, "Who do you work for?" I answered, "I work for myself."

Finally, I had found the right answer, and as a result my view of resources shifted dramatically. Whether we work for someone or are off on our own, seeing *ourselves* as the person we work for will light a fire under us to identify the resources *we* can access, rather than waiting for buckets of money to appear through venture capital coups or budget allocations.

WHAT ARE YOUR RESOURCES?

Now that you know who you work for, you need to take an honest look at two things: what your resources are right now and where they can take you.

I currently drive an Audi A6. I love this car, and I love going on road trips in it. No matter the distance or destination, I know I'm going to get there, and I know I'll travel in comfort. I can sing along with my favorite music on the satellite radio, and my biggest worry is that my speed will creep up to the point where I'll get a ticket. Driving this car is an absolute pleasure!

My Audi A6 is dramatically different from what I drove in college. When my wife and I were first married, we drove a 1972 Dodge Colt that had been wrecked three times. I know people joke about cars that are held together with bailing wire and duct tape, but ours actually was. We tried to improve its appearance by covering up some of the larger dents with a rough coat of Bondo and then painting the entire car with blue spray paint. That plan didn't work very well. In fact, I was so embarrassed by the car that when I was working on my MBA,

I would park half a mile away so that no one would see what I drove. The car had a broken oil pan, and the head was cracked. It would get me to school and back, but I never dared take it out on the freeway, let alone on a road trip.

Back then, that was my only resource for getting to my destination. I can go a lot farther now in my Audi A6 than I could in that old Dodge Colt. But the Colt was better than my eight-year-old son's current resources. He recently founded a business selling homemade crafts around the neighborhood. When he makes his deliveries, his mode of transportation is a kick scooter. So, while my Dodge Colt was constrained by the city limits, his radius is a few blocks from our home. But he is making do with the resources at his disposal. His vehicle is different from my Audi A6 and even my Dodge Colt. But it can still take him places.

Of course, the business he is building with his resources is dramatically different than the type of businesses I am able to build. But then, the businesses I build are dramatically different than the ones Donald Trump builds. Which is why he has a jet!

Obviously, we can go farther if we have a jet than if we just have a kick scooter. But any one of these vehicles will get us somewhere. We may have farther to go and more zigs and zags to create if we are starting with the kick scooter, but even when we think we have no resources, we actually do. Whatever your circumstances, it is important to look deep down in your pockets.

I grew up in a rural southern Utah town with a population of about 2,000, if you include the cows and chickens. My family did not have any worldly wealth to speak of. But I had dreams of going to college, succeeding as an engineer and businessman, and moving somewhere a bit bigger than my beloved hometown. When I was a young boy, my resources were the equivalent of my son's kick scooter. They consisted mainly of sheer determination, the guts to move forward, time, and boundless energy. I also had a bicycle, which was handy because a nice neighbor who knew I wanted to work offered me a paper route. With that paper route, I was able to save enough money to fix up an old lawn mower that was sitting unused in our shed. After a bit of self-promotion, another neighbor offered me the job of mowing the hospital's lawns. Between the paper route and the lawn mowing, I was able to buy more lawn mowers, and I invited my brothers to help mow other lawns. I kept a percentage of what they earned, which seemed fair because I was supplying the equipment. I saved most of the money I earned and put it toward my goal of going to college. I also worked hard in high school and received a scholarship, which added more resources toward my goal to graduate from college.

It may seem that I traveled in a fairly straight line toward my goal, but if you look more carefully, I did a lot of zigging and zagging. It may also seem that I had very limited resources, but let's review them before arriving at that conclusion:

⇨ Determination

⇨ Time

⇨ Energy

⇨ Good health

⇨ Supportive parents

⇨ A bicycle

⇨ A neighbor who offered me a paper route

⇨ An old lawn mower in the shed

⇨ Money to fix the lawn mower

⇨ Knowledge to fix the lawn mower

⇨ Another neighbor who offered me the lawn-mowing job

⇨ Friends who wanted to mow lawns

⇨ Good grades, which led to a scholarship

I love speaking to young, enthusiastic college students. But whenever I talk about resources, one of them will say, "Rich, it's great you've been able to start all these businesses, but look at where you are!" I then have to tell them that I had to climb the ladder, rung by rung, starting at the very bottom.

MENTAL CAPITAL

I value education. I grew up determined to graduate from college, and I did. Twice. First, I earned a bachelor's degree in electronic engineering (which is not a major I would recommend if you want to sail through college), and second, I earned an MBA.

I give you this background because I don't want you to misunderstand when I say that getting an MBA or any other degree is not mental capital. Information alone is not sufficient. I know enough "educated idiots" who are very book smart but are not able to put what they've learned to good use. Whether your sources of information are traditional or nontraditional, your mental capital is your ability to apply that information.

I learned things in my MBA program that have been of direct benefit—lessons having to do with finances, human resources, motivational philosophies, and so on. But the greatest benefits came from experiencing the discipline of learning—exploring, digging, experimenting, and applying. I made it a point to continue to explore and discover after I received my diploma, and I've learned some lessons since that have stayed with me far longer than the content I was tested on in the classroom.

As you assess your mental capital, by all means consider what you've learned in school, but also consider what you're good at. What special skills do you have that you could apply to your current situation? What are you curious about? Do you have unique insight or understanding about a particular field?

For me, I think I have some natural ability as a salesman, which helped me convince my brothers to mow lawns for me. I'm good at understanding technology, something I was aware of when I set out to repair that old lawnmower in my parents' garage. Both are forms of mental capital I've continued to use to this day. Somewhere in my career, I became adept at search-engine optimization, or making sure websites show up at the top of the list you see when you push "search." That knowledge didn't exist when I graduated from college, but I picked it up along the road and it's paid big dividends.

I have an acquaintance who had a solid career in print journalism at the time personal computers first made their appearance back in the early 1980s. Like everyone around him, he had to learn a new set of skills. Some of his coworkers balked at the changes this new technology was bringing to the newsroom and did as little as humanly possible to adapt. But Bob got excited, learned all he could, dug deeper than most, then kept digging, and today oversees a vast and complex website for an international organization.

I know another man who didn't quite finish his degree in graphic design, in part because he needed to get a job to support a growing family. He had worked for a small television station as a student and was able to get on full-time when he dropped out of college. Rather than feeling he was at a dead end, though, he taught himself everything he could about a technology that was shifting from analog to digital and from standard definition to high definition. Soon he became indispensable to the organization, and a few years later he caught the eye of a major television studio that needed someone who could keep pace with systems that change almost daily. It was not a degree that got him this higher paying job, it was his mental capital.

Sometimes our schools present learning as a straight line: you learn this, you pass the test on that, you get your diploma, you get your first job, and you move up the ranks. But identifying and applying our mental capital will inevitably lead us to zigs and zags throughout our lives, if we are willing to open our eyes to our potential and to the possibilities that lie before us.

Passion is a vital form of mental capital. It not only drives us, but it gets people aligned with us as we pursue our goals. In my professional pursuits, I am passionate about technology and about building businesses. Now, technology can be a pretty dry subject, but I can almost guarantee you I'll bring so much passion to any discussion we have that you'll find yourself fascinated before long. Recently, I was given one hour to meet with an internationally known figure to discuss a technology I thought might benefit him. The one hour he agreed to turned into four hours, and at the end of our discussion he introduced me to his colleagues by proclaiming, "This is the *coolest* geek I've ever met!"

Your passions will be different from mine. But find them. Make sure your own fire is burning brightly, and others will see it and support you in your pursuits.

RELATIONSHIP CAPITAL

If you take your smarts and your intelligence and do nothing but sit in a dark room and think about how bright you are, then obviously nothing is going to come of them. But if you take your smarts and your intelligence and use them to the benefit of people around you, the relationships you build will propel you toward your goals. Likely, you won't find yourself traveling in a straight line, but, even with twists and turns, you'll get there.

While I was still in college, I worked in technical support for a startup company named Netline. Everyone in the company was busting their guts to make this little leading-edge technology business work, and we had advanced to the point where we had attracted the attention of a billionaire who was coming to see if he wanted to invest in the company.

The day before he was to arrive, we set up a demo wall and prepared everything needed to show him the technology. I was just a peon in this company, but as I was getting ready to leave that night, I noticed our cement floor had not been swept or mopped, and the place was filthy. We were a startup, and we were so focused on the technology that those small details were overlooked. But I guess I had learned enough from my mother to feel embarrassed to have this incredibly successful businessman see our offices looking as they did.

So I drove home and got my wife, and we went back and cleaned the building. As it happened, everyone was gone by the time we started, and the next day I didn't feel any need to point out what we had done.

We made our presentation to the businessman, he was impressed with the technology, and the company got the funding it needed. As we celebrated, there was a buzz about who had cleaned the building; and even though I didn't say anything, someone figured out who had corrected a glaring oversight. As simple as my contribution was, it created relationship capital with the vice president of marketing, who asked me to be his technician. Before long, he was promoting me within the company and inviting me to travel with him to trade shows.

I didn't have much mental capital at that point, but— without even intending to do so—I formed relationships that have lasted for years, simply by knowing which end of a broom to hold on to.

Several years ago I traveled to Lake Tahoe to deliver a lecture. Before the appointed time, I had the opportunity to meet with a group of about 20 young entrepreneurs from Canada who had asked if I'd spend an hour with them answering questions on starting businesses.

We had a delightful exchange, and, as we got to the end of our time together, they asked me what they could do to help me. Not thinking anything about it, I said something like, "Oh, everything's good. Thanks for the offer." As I was heading to the presentation I had come to make, one of my associates told me we had misplaced the handouts we were going to use. He was a little panicked and was hoping we could find a copy machine in time to make new copies.

The next thing that I knew, Ernistina, one of the young Canadians, had gathered her team together. They figured out where to make the photocopies and then took the time to hand them out to the group of people who were gathered in the lecture hall. Because of her awareness and service, the event went off without any glitches and was a success. I was so grateful to Ernistina that I instantly invited her to a seminar we were teaching on entrepreneurship. We, of course, waived the tuition and even helped with her travel expenses.

Ernistina certainly hadn't met with me with the plan that she could then turn her energies toward making photocopies, and I can only assume that she had other things to do after we finished our discussion. But by being willing to serve me, she was able to expand her relationship capital considerably. And I was able to make a new friend.

Building networks of relationships does not happen overnight, and it takes attentiveness and hard work. I've seen people who set out with a very clear goal to build a network as quickly as possible. They see their goal, and they see others as a way to reach the goal. And they often bulldoze straight ahead, leaving expendable bodies in their wake. Some of the greatest relationships I've been fortunate to enjoy have come at the end of zigzagging that took place over months and even years—and could never have been envisioned if I had sat down and tried to map out who I needed to know and where knowing them would get me.

As part of my MBA program while I was still working at Novell, I had the opportunity to go on a trip through Asia to study various businesses in Japan, Korea, and China. When I returned, Mitsubishi had just signed a contract with Novell for some strategic engineering work. As it happened, I was the only one in our department who had ever been to Japan. So, even though I did not speak the language, I got assigned to be the strategic engineer for Mitsubishi.

During this time the president of Mitsubishi's PC Division, Dr. Peter Horne, traveled from Japan to Utah several times to meet with Novell's CEO, Ray Noorda. My job was to pick him up at the Salt Lake City airport and drive him to our Provo office, which was about an hour away. I suppose I could have viewed this assignment as something of a chore, but I chose to see it as an opportunity to get to know a very bright, talented, capable individual. So, I washed my car (thank goodness, I had recently traded up from the Dodge Colt!) and tried to think of some interesting topics of conversation.

Dr. Horne and I had made the same trip several times when something happened that changed my life. As he climbed into my car on a Wednesday afternoon for another trip back to the airport, Dr. Horne tossed his jacket into the back seat of my car, unbeknownst to me. When we pulled up to the terminal, he grabbed his luggage but inadvertently left his jacket behind. I drove home, dropped off the car for my wife, and then got a ride to a Boy Scout activity I was helping to chaperone.

This was before cell phones, and while I was gone my wife got a frantic call from Dr. Horne letting her know that he had failed to retrieve his jacket and that his passport and wallet were in its pockets. Without a second thought, my wife loaded our three kids (all under the age of six) into the car and drove like crazy up to the airport. My wife and these little kids ran through the airport as fast as they could in order to get the jacket to Dr. Horne before his flight took off. (If you can remember ancient history, this was before the days of airport security.)

A few weeks later my wife received a package in the mail with a beautiful hand-carved jewelry box and a thank-you note. In the note Dr. Horne commented that his wallet had contained a substantial amount of cash and that not one cent had been touched. He expressed amazement that we would have the integrity to return his wallet without even looking inside. He was also grateful that my wife would drive up, even though it was clearly an inconvenience. In a subsequent conversation, Dr. Horne told me that if I ever decided to leave Novell, he would like to talk with me. Indeed, the time did come when I left Novell, and through a series of fortuitous events I became the general manager of Mitsubishi Electrics PC Division in the United States. Meeting Dr. Horne was one of the first real breaks I had during the early years of my career. What started out as a small act of service on my wife's part was rewarded with a strong mentor, boss, and a dear friend. I will be forever grateful to Dr. Peter Horne.

Building relationships is an important and never-ending opportunity that will set the foundation for your zigzagging. It will open more doors for you than you could ever imagine. It's also a process that needs to be looked at from the right perspective. I would recommend that you remember two important principles: First, do the right things for the right reasons. Second, don't ever use people.

We live in a selfish world where some people believe the world stopped revolving around the sun on the day they were born. Some have the mindset that everyone but themselves is disposable and that they can just burn through as many people as necessary to get where they're going. My experience and observations have taught me repeatedly that a far better way to live is to have a genuine concern for others and seek ways to serve those around you. That said, our motivation should never be anything other than doing the right thing.

I recall one young man who I was eager to help. He was incredibly bright and talented, and I saw a lot of potential in him. On several occasions I put myself out there to help him. When I was leaving the department where I had been his boss, I made sure he had a good position. A few weeks later, he complained to me that he was not happy in his new job and was looking for another. I opened my network of friends to him and helped him find new employment. A couple of months later he had burned through those relationships, and I found myself having to apologize to close associates for the messes he had created. I recommended him for several other jobs and offered my advice whenever he called. I even helped him get into a prestigious MBA school.

I never received a thank-you from him, nor any offer to reciprocate for the help I had given him. In fact, one time I asked a very small favor of him, but he was too busy. Another time I overheard him pointing out some of my weaknesses to a group of associates. We should not help others with an eye toward what we can get in return, but when all we get back is a lack of gratitude and a sense of being used, that becomes burdensome. In this case, though my "friend" continued to call for help from time to time, I simply quit responding to his demands and returning his calls. No one likes to feel used.

APPLICATION

Wherever you are and whatever you plan to do, you'll benefit from making a list of the resources you have at your disposal. Start with what you have today and dig deep down into your pocket. Look for resources that you might otherwise overlook.

VALUE EQUATION

MENTAL CAPITAL + RELATIONSHIP CAPITAL =
FINANCIAL CAPITAL

VALUE EQUATION
1. LIST YOUR MENTAL CAPITAL: WHAT ARE YOU GOOD AT? WHAT ARE YOU PASSIONATE ABOUT? WHAT SKILLS DO YOU HAVE?
2. LIST YOUR RELATIONSHIP CAPITAL: WHO ARE 10 PEOPLE THAT CAN HELP YOU GET CLOSER TO YOUR GOALS?
3. IF YOU DO NOT HAVE 10 PEOPLE YOU CAN CALL ON, WHAT CAN YOU DO TO BUILD RELATIONSHIPS WITH 10 SUCH PEOPLE? HOW CAN YOU SERVE THESE PEOPLE?

EATING OUR OWN COOKING

Throughout this book, I will provide proof from my own experience that the principles I'm putting forth work. So, to summarize our need to identify our resources—which should include a combination of mental capital and relationship capital—here's an introduction to the company I will be using to prove the points of this book. This company's name is Froghair. I'll return to it in each of the chapters that follow.

In 2001, I was running a technology company and had a very bright employee named Abbie Hunter. She was an aggressive young woman who had dreams of her own and who told me one day that she wanted me to help her set up a company. And she meant it! After thinking through what I'd be willing to get involved with I said, "Okay, Abbie, I'll help you with whatever idea you come up with, but it has to involve the outdoors and golf." Why? Because I had plans to go climbing in the Himalayas, and I am also an avid golfer. I figured if I was going to add anything to an already very full plate, it had better be something I was passionate about.

Abbie went to work on ideas and a few weeks later came back with a business plan involving selling outdoor and golf equipment. I agreed to combine my mental and relationship capital with hers, and we started a company with almost zero financial capital.

Well, the business did okay and we had some fun working on it, but it was not a high priority for me or for Abbie, and eventually she left to take a well-deserved job on the East Coast. I was now on my own with it, and it turned into something my boys and I ran out of our garage. Orders would come in; the boys would label, clean, and pack the products; and then semitrucks would pull into our small neighborhood to pick up the orders. One time I actually slept in the garage to keep my eye on a particularly large order. I had fun and scored some nice equipment, my boys learned some good lessons and discipline, but the business was never something my wife and I used to feed our family.

A couple of years into this, I developed a relationship with Curtis Blair, who shared my passion for golf. He had experience and knowledge of the golf market. He also had knowledge of Latin America and spoke Spanish. He decided he wanted in on this deal (maybe for the free golf balls?), so we agreed that he'd come on board to develop markets in Central and South America and expand the corporate side of the business, which he did with considerable success. We were able to combine our mental capital and relationship capital to establish a small stable of commercial accounts with whom we made a point of maintaining very strong relationships. We also built relationships with several high-end, name-brand suppliers, all of which loved doing business with us because we *always* paid our bills on time, often well in advance of what their terms called for. (The know-how and understanding of the need to build strong relationships is part of my mental capital.)

The company grew to the point where, when we wanted to get out from under it, we were able to sell it for a tidy profit. However, we cared about the relationships we had formed during our years together, so we were very careful about screening the buyer, who turned out to be a man in Arizona who had an abundance of financial capital and a similar passion for golf. His idea for running the company, though, was that he would turn the operations over to a college student and our buyer would leave town for a month at a time to play golf. The outcome of his brilliant business plan was a disaster, which might surprise some people because the man we sold the business to had all the financial capital needed to take our gem of an idea and make it a huge success!

Not that we wanted it, but when the new owner fell behind in the payments he owed us, Curtis and I ended up taking back our ownership in 2009. Gratefully, we still had our relationships with suppliers and clients, we understood the markets and business processes, and we hadn't lost any of our passion for being outdoors and playing too much golf. The one change we did make was that we renamed the company "Froghair" and then set out to achieve our long-term goals (which I'll share in the next chapter).

There was a lot of zigzagging involved when I first started that company with Abbie. There was a lot more when Curtis joined up with me and took us into markets I didn't know anything about. And there was even more when we regained ownership. But that zigzagging was possible because we identified our mental and relationship capital.

SUMMARY

Whether you're looking to start your own company, to excel in the company you work for, or to achieve goals in your personal life that have always eluded you, the first step in building your foundation is assessing your resources. Just as Donald Trump's jet can fly him around the world, my Audi can easily get me across the country, and my son's kick scooter can get him down the block, we can each start with what we have right now, and then decide where we want to go with our own unique vehicle. Then we can trade up as we acquire more resources.

Now that you've begun identifying your resources, it's time to learn about setting your beacon in the fog.

Beacons in the Fog and Catalyzing Statements

Midway through my career, I was working for an incredibly shrewd and successful businessman named Ladd Christensen. One day, in a moment of frustration, he called me into his office and bellowed, "Rich, define 'entrepreneurship'!"

I rattled off some lame textbook answer, and he responded, "Wrong. Wrong! Entrepreneurship is having the courage to wander in the fog."

At the time I didn't really buy it. My style was to move from point A to point B in as direct a line as possible. I was (and still am) a goal setter, and wandering aimlessly held no appeal; in fact, it seemed antithetical to getting where I wanted to go, either in business or in life.

Although I disagreed strongly with Ladd at the time, the point of his tirade became much more clear years later when I read an article by a well-known educator and religious leader who told how he had once asked for clarity from his file leader on an assignment and received what initially seemed to be a puzzling response:

> He [told me], "The trouble with you is you want to see the end from the beginning." I replied that [yes] I would like to see at least a step or two ahead. Then came the lesson of a lifetime: "You must learn to walk to the edge of the light, and then a few steps into the darkness; then the light will appear and show the way before you."
>
> (Boyd K. Packer, "The Edge of the Light," BYU Today, March 1991)

Despite my natural inclination to always want to know exactly where I'm headed, I've learned that, whether we're talking about starting a business, completing a complex project our boss has given us, or helping a trying teen get through high school, our lives inevitably involve some wandering in the fog. Very seldom do we have a crystal ball showing us every step we should take and everything that is going to happen.

FINDING OUR BEACON IN THE FOG

It is one thing to wander aimlessly, which some of us, unfortunately, do. It's a very different matter to identify and set our sights on what I call a big, audacious goal, which becomes our "beacon in the fog." With that beacon firmly in mind, we are far better equipped to head into the darkness, knowing we may not always be able to see where we're going with crystal clarity, but still know where we're headed. Airline pilots do this all the time. They barrel through storms and massive cloud banks at 500 miles per hour, unable to see 10 feet in front of them, and we passengers are accepting of this insanity because we know they are fixed on a clearly identified bearing.

If we're smart, we do the same thing. We start out with a big goal to guide us, and every once in a while we hit a smaller goal, which provides a break in the fog that lets us catch sight of our beacon before we take those next steps into the darkness. The process is more messy and risky than it is clean, pristine, planned, and calculated. But if you have a solid, clearly defined beacon in the fog to move toward—and a foundation to travel on—then you will arrive at your destination, just as you've planned. *But only after some inevitable zigzagging!*

In the last chapter, you assessed your resources and figured out what kind of vehicle you have at your disposal to take on your journey to success. Now let's talk about clearly identifying your destination. Where do you want to go? What is your beacon in the fog?

Imagine there are two groups of friends who want to take a trip, and both groups start out with identical resources. The first group spends considerable time researching travel ideas on the Internet. As they explore various options, each mentions a long-held dream of seeing France, so they set a goal to travel there together in one year. When their income tax returns arrive, each person deposits the money in a special fund created just for this trip. They cut expenses wherever they can in order to build their savings accounts. They each get a credit card that gives them double miles, which they then use responsibly (so they're not wasting the money they're saving on interest). They even put their change in a jar at the end of the day.

A year later, they are able to purchase their airline tickets with frequent flyer miles; in fact, they have enough miles to upgrade to those oversized business-class seats with the individual video amenities. Soon after, they are ready to take off. They fly into the Charles de Gaulle Airport, then head to the luxurious Hotel de Crillon. While in Paris, they schedule adequate time to stroll through the Louvre and see some of the world's most famous paintings. Of course, the Mona Lisa is at the top of the list. They climb to the top of the Eiffel Tower, counting each step as they go. Their evenings are spent in famous French restaurants that serve croissant au beurre, thinly sliced French fries, and sweet crepes. After enjoying Paris, they make their way down the beautiful French Riviera to visit Nice and Cannes. They even take a day trip to Monaco to visit the raceway and winding streets that meander along the sheer cliffs. After spending two weeks of leisurely, deliberate enjoyment, they return home, relaxing in business class.

The other group of friends kind of jump in their car one day and say, "Hey, let's take a trip!" Once they're all in, they open their wallets and see they have a total of $17.93 among them. That doesn't seem like much, but one person has a credit card with a $500 credit line (at 29 percent interest). No one has a strong opinion about where to go, so they flip a coin to see if they should travel east or west. The quarter lands on tails, so they head west. As they leave town, they stop at the local Gas-n-Go to fill up and buy some snacks and soda pop. They charge the credit card for the gas and drinks, and off they go. After about 200 miles, they realize they are in a remote part of Northern Nevada, where the inhabitants consist mostly of rabbits and rattlesnakes. Not surprisingly, they realize they have no idea where the closest town is, which concerns them because their gas tank is getting low and they are almost out of drinks. Suddenly, they begin praying that they have enough snacks and gas to get them back home. And, in the midst of those silent prayers, they find they are getting on each other's nerves.

In both cases, these are trips that are going to be talked about for years to come. But the nature of the reminiscences will vary considerably!

Many people live their lives much like the friends who took the second road trip. They take whatever comes and live day-to-day or paycheck-to-paycheck. They do not have a plan or a goal for where they want to go, let alone end up. There is no beacon guiding them toward where they have determined they want to go.

Finding your beacon is a very personal and individual pursuit, but there are some principles that should guide you.

First, you should look for those things you are passionate about and you have the ability to achieve. They should exceed your grasp so that you're pushed, but they should not be so far beyond your reach that they are unattainable.

In *The Seven Habits of Highly Effective People,* Stephen R. Covey talks about our areas of influence and areas of concern. We all have things in our lives where our preferences and choices can and do make a difference. These are our areas of influence. Some are quite simple. For example, what we wear to work, what we eat for breakfast, or even the jobs we choose to apply for are all things that are clearly within our area of influence. Then there are areas that are more complex, but where we certainly do have an influence. If we're part of a management team, we may not have complete control over decisions that are made, but we do have a say. If we're a parent, we can't really force our children to do exactly what we want, but we can certainly influence their behaviors. If we see a compelling social need, we may not be able to solve it single-handedly, but we can make our own unique contribution.

Then there are those things that, no matter what our concerns may be, are not within our area of influence. Because I love being outdoors, I am very concerned about the weather. But, no matter how vocal I may be when I wake up wanting to play golf and find snow on the ground, there is not a darned thing I can do about it. If I work at the lowest staff level of an international conglomerate, I likely will have no real influence on corporate strategies. If I own a small manufacturing business, the price of gas is beyond my control, even though it has a huge impact on my business plan and profits.

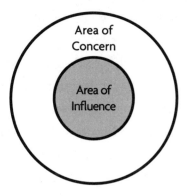

Most people spend 80 percent of their time worrying about things they cannot control. In other words, they spend all of their time and energy focusing on their areas of concern rather than their area of influence. The way to identify those things you want to pursue is to focus right on the border of where your area of influence touches your area of concern. If you establish your beacon in the fog right on the edge of your area of influence, you will find that your area of influence becomes much larger and you will find that your goals, though challenging, actually are achievable.

If we're not setting goals that are within our reach as part of finding our beacon, we will find ourselves doing a lot of aimless wandering in the fog. I've always been motivated by the goals I've set; in fact, every year I see to it that my family gets together and makes goals. These are not your garden-variety New Year's resolutions; these are actual goals we plan to achieve, individually and collectively. We make short-term goals, mid-term goals, and long-term goals. (Personally, I have already set goals through the end of my life.) It has been fun to see the kinds of goals our children come up with each year.

We do not judge each other's goals. We just write them down and post them on the refrigerator. As the year progresses and each goal is met, the children ceremoniously cross off each goal, which brings a huge sense of satisfaction. Sometimes we will put up goals that are a big stretch to reach. Other goals might be much simpler. Over the years my family has found that the best way to make goals is to keep three things in mind. A goal needs to be: (1) written down, (2) measurable, and (3) realistic. It never ceases to amaze me how powerful this simple process of creating and writing down goals ends up being. Of course, times change, priorities shift, and we all do our fair share of zigzagging toward our goals. So while there are a few goals that end up not being completed, most of what we've committed to gets crossed off by the end of the year. What I find more gratifying than just checking off goals is seeing how my children's goals provide them with direction and motivation throughout the year.

I'll admit there have been times when a family member's goals have left me wondering how they were ever going to achieve them. But I've also seen many examples of how having that beacon in the fog provides a powerful reminder and sense of purpose. A few years ago, my seven-year-old son had us write down a goal that really made me chuckle. When we asked him what goals he wanted to pursue, without hesitation he blurted out, "I want to go chicken chasing!" We all laughed; but, in keeping with family policy, we wrote it down and posted it on the fridge.

Now, neither do we live anywhere near a farm nor do we have any chickens nearby, so my wife and I were not sure how this goal was going to be met. I suppose we could have driven him to a petting zoo, but in reality his achieving this goal was not a big priority for my wife or me. When we did think about it, we just figured this would be a goal that would sit on the list and at the end of the year we would say, "Well, sorry, but that one just didn't happen."

The year progressed, and of course there was no chicken chasing. In fact, we thought he had forgotten all about his goal. Then one day in mid-October, my wife called me on the phone, laughing uncontrollably. She and our kids had stopped at the post office to pick up some mail. As they got back in the car, the son who wanted to chase chickens got really excited. He and his younger brother then bolted out of the car and started chasing two wild roosters that had been sitting in the bushes at the post office. My wife and the older brothers watched as these two little boys chased those birds around for a good five minutes. My son was so excited when he got home that the first thing he did was grab his big red crayon and cross off "Chicken Chasing" from his list of goals.

While you may never have a goal of chasing chickens, my son's experience exemplifies the power of identifying and then writing down those things that are going to serve as our beacons in the fog. While everyone else in our family had pretty much forgotten about his goal, he kept looking toward that beacon—and for the right opportunity to achieve his goal. I have found that if you put a goal out there and write it down, it is amazing what the universe will return to you.

Your beacons in the fog are generally longer-term goals that your short-term and mid-term goals will lead you toward. You can have several beacons you are working toward in different areas of your life. When I began college, I had identified several beacons in the fog I intended to pursue. One was to graduate from college. Another was to meet the woman I would marry. Still another was to find significant ways to render service. I must say that the day I started college, I had no idea how I was going to accomplish those goals, but those beacons provided me with guidance and motivation as I developed the short-term and mid-term goals that kept me moving toward the light.

After graduating from college (and accomplishing my other two goals), I came up with a new set of beacons that centered around building a strong family, finding success in my career, continuing my education, and finding additional ways to serve. As I've found myself approaching 50, I've wanted to find an additional beacon that would motivate and guide me in ways that transcend the businesses I've been involved in building and the financial goals I've established for myself and my family.

Finding that beacon took quite some time, but as I searched for it, I realized I have always been concerned about the plight of the poverty-stricken women and children around the world. It just dismays me to see the starving children and the abuses of women in developing countries. I have traveled in some of these countries, and I watch the news and worry about these people so much that I set a rather general goal of helping women in emerging countries find their way out of poverty. However, I felt for a long time that this was a goal that was largely out of my area of influence.

Many experiences have helped me change my view, but perhaps none more powerfully than when I had the opportunity to interview a man named Steve Comrie, who is a pioneer in the satellite television industry. He and his business partner, David Reid, have both been very successful in their field. At one point, the two somehow became aligned with Afghanistan and discovered a group of freedom fighters who desperately wanted to bring honest, fair, and open television to the Afghanis.

Over time, this goal became Steve and Dave's beacon in the fog, despite the realities they faced in dealing with a corrupt government, Taliban strongholds, and many others who were hostile to the idea of a free flow of information. As they undertook this endeavor, the two men spent many weeks and months having no idea how they would find their way through the darkness. But they had a goal in mind, and through a series of miraculous events, Steve and Dave made the decision to go to Afghanistan to play their part in helping these freedom fighters. At great personal risk, they were able to set up uncensored television programming. They even created a program called *The Mask,* in which Afghan women who usually have no voice in social issues can wear a mask and speak freely about what is happening in their country without fear of reprisal or death.

Was this undertaking at the very edge of Steve and Dave's comfort zone? Indeed it was. It was also right on the fringe of their area of influence and their area of concern. But through identifying and pursuing their beacon in the fog, they have been able to expand their area of influence, and they are actually doing something about their area of concern. Their undertaking meant they had to spend considerable time zigzagging through the fog guided by their beacon, but in the process they did something remarkable for the women and the men of Afghanistan.

I contend that all the great breakthroughs that occur in the world happen when people act right on the perimeter of their area of influence and their area of concern. This is where real power and influence is born.

Catalyzing Statements

Soon after John F. Kennedy became president, he began to see the importance of the manned space program that President Dwight D. Eisenhower had envisioned; in fact, in his State of the Union address in January 1961, he made his support of manned space flight clear. Then on April 12, 1961, the Soviet Union sent the first man into space, which seemed to show the world that while the United States had dreams and ambitions, it was lagging behind in achieving its goal.

President Kennedy did not want to fall behind the Soviet Union, which was putting more money and effort toward space than we were at that time. So, on May 25, 1961, he stood before a special joint session of Congress and outlined what could be viewed as his beacon in the fog. He said:

I believe we possess all the resources and talents necessary. But the facts of the matter are that we have never made the national decisions or marshaled the national resources required for such leadership [in space travel]. We have never specified long-range goals on an urgent time schedule, or managed our resources and our time so as to ensure their fulfillment.

It's important to note that President Kennedy did not stop there. Instead, President Kennedy added what my associate Rick Sapio refers to as a catalyzing statement when he said:

I believe that this nation should commit itself to achieving the goal, before this decade is out, of landing a man on the moon and returning him safely to the earth.

(Special address to the United States Congress, May 25, 1961.)

Of course, that goal was fulfilled when on July 20, 1969, less than a decade after President Kennedy made his famous speech, Neil Armstrong did indeed walk on the moon and returned to earth safely.

Catalyzing statements add specificity and are the fuel that motivates us—and those around us—to keep moving toward our beacon in the fog.

At the risk of sounding immodest, I would say that my beacon in the fog of helping people in developing countries is noble, but it is also too broad. This leads to two problems. The first is that, even though I have a goal, it lacks any specificity to guide my actions day to day. The second is that, as I try to garner support from others, my goal seems overwhelming and unattainable.

So, I refined my goal and concluded I wanted to help educate youth from around the world. Even with that, though, it still lacked focus and was too vague for others to grasp. Eventually, I arrived at my catalyzing statement, which is: "I plan on educating 1,000 youth from around the world before I turn 50." That was the point when I became very focused and also found others who were willing to support my dream. Suddenly doors opened and opportunities arose that helped lead us closer to this goal.

On a very different scale, what I did was much the same as when John F. Kennedy declared, "We will get a man on the moon before the end of the decade . . . and return him home safely." We must clearly identify our beacon in the fog, and then we must follow that up by creating our catalyzing statement.

As I've come to understand and apply the concepts of beacons in the fog and catalyzing statements, I've watched to see if others who have achieved significant success follow the same pattern. An associate of mine was central to helping a small, Rocky Mountain company grow from a family business to a major commercial construction corporation. As I asked my associate about how the company grew, he shared a very telling story.

Back in the late 1980s, he was attending a conference with several of his key executives. The speaker asked the question, "Who has a mission statement for their company?" My associate raised his hand, but the speaker didn't ask him what the mission statement was. Instead, he asked if any of the company's executive staff were in attendance. Some were, so the speaker asked the executives, "What is your company's mission statement?" These individuals stuttered and stammered and could not recite it. It was an embarrassing moment, and these executives were very apologetic. My associate then wrestled with what he could use to clarify the company's purpose and unify his executives around it. He settled on the phrase: *Constructing with Integrity.*

He then went on to explain in detail what that mantra meant:

1. What we produce: Build using the highest level of quality and not cut corners. Use the best materials and the best methodologies available to construct with integrity.

2. How we deal with people: Behave ethically and treat all people equally and with respect. Construct relationships with integrity.

3. The organization we build: Remove posturing and politics and build our organization and interactions with each other with respect. Construct the organization with integrity.

These simple three words—Constructing with Integrity— became the North Star, the guiding beacon, for this construction company. What grew out of this beacon was the company's emotional fuel, or catalyzing statements. And, as my associate told me, "Everyone understood what we stood for, and it was very rewarding."

Some time later, at a company function, someone took a camera around and began asking team members what *Constructing with Integrity* meant to them. Here are a few of the statements from that day:

"It means I can live the same way on the job as when I am at home with my wife."

"It means I don't ever have to apologize to anyone for the quality of work we do."

"It means I can be honest with my boss and with my direct reports about what it will take to do a job right."

Catalyzing statements go way beyond articulating a goal. They emotionally charge us and align us. They internally motivate us to seek and believe and move forward.

Another good example of the power found in a broad goal with a catalyzing statement involves Bill Gates. In the early days of Microsoft, he would boldly declare, "We're going to become the largest software company in the world!" That sounded great, but at that time nobody even knew what software was! Was Gates referring to a pair of snuggly, warm pajamas? No one could really wrap their heads around what he was saying. Then one day he made the statement, "I picture a world where there is a personal computer in every home and on every desktop." That was something people understood, and it became Microsoft's catalyzing statement. The rest, of course, is history. And, just like John F. Kennedy or Bill Gates, your catalyzing statement needs to be something you use as your emotional fuel that can rally the troops.

Several years ago I was in Japan, and I had the opportunity to visit a company in Tokyo called Fujita. From the moment I entered this company's headquarters, I knew it was unique. The tone, the conduct of the staff, and the presentation of the boardroom were simply different. It was very clear that everyone was focused and clearly on a mission. At the end of our meeting I could not help but probe a bit, so I asked the individual I was meeting with to explain more about the company, its founder, and its history. His answer was immediate and brief—and it told me everything I was looking for. He simply said, "Fujita's vision is to bring American culture to Japan."

Now that is a powerful, huge, audacious, and crazy goal. "Bring American culture to Japan!"

Fujita's daily activities include selling hamburgers, movies, clothing, and other products, most of which are imported. But those things are simply vehicles in support of Fujita's catalyzing statement. And that catalyzing statement has resulted in Fujita bringing McDonald's, Blockbuster, and Toys"R"Us to Japan.

DISCOVERING YOUR OWN BEACON

We humans were not designed to sit back and be idle. We are wired to push ourselves to do things of great significance. Steve Jobs made this point in a commencement speech he delivered at Stanford in 2005:

> *You've got to find what you love. And that is as true for your work as it is for your lovers. Your work is going to fill a large part of your life, and the only way to be truly satisfied is to do what you believe is great work. And the only way to do great work is to love what you do. If you haven't found it yet, keep looking. Don't settle. As with all matters of the heart, you'll know when you find it. And, like any great relationship, it just gets better and better as the years roll on. So keep looking until you find it. Don't settle.*
>
> *("'You've got to find what you love,' Jobs says."*
> Stanford Report, *June 14, 2005.)*

52

Goals are what will give you direction as you encounter the fog and darkness that is so much a part of life. Catalyzing statements are what will provide you motivation and fuel as you pursue your beacon in the fog.

To help you identify your beacons in the fog and your attendant catalyzing statements, I want you to complete the following model that Garrett Gunderson has developed (and which I use with his permission). As you work through it, you will find those goals that are unique to you and that will motivate you in ways you might have thought impossible.

First complete the Soul Purpose Finder on page 54. Then review your answers while looking for trends and similarities. Evaluate which talents, passions, activities, and/or interests appeared more than once and then circle them. You will then take those and enter them on the spokes of your Soul Purpose Wheel below. A wheel signifies motion, and that's

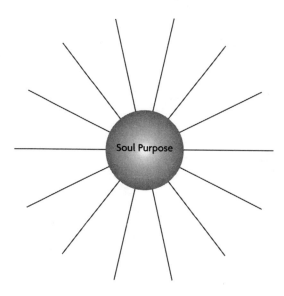

SOUL PURPOSE FINDER
1. I'M HAPPIEST WHEN
2. I'M MOST CREATIVE WHEN
3. WHAT DOES AN IDEAL LIFE LOOK LIKE FOR ME?
4. WHAT ACTIVITIES MAKE ME EXCITED TO GET UP IN THE MORNING?
5. THE THINGS I AM MOST PASSIONATE ABOUT IN LIFE ARE
6. WHEN DO I FEEL THAT I AM LIVING MY PURPOSE?
7. WHAT HOBBIES/INTERESTS DO I HAVE THAT COULD POTENTIALLY CROSS OVER AS INCOME?
8. WHAT TALENTS/ATTRIBUTES DO I REGULARLY GET COMPLIMENTED ON?
9. WHAT TALENTS OR ACTIVITIES THAT I ENJOY AM I CURRENTLY BEING PAID FOR?
10. WHAT AREAS/ACTIVITIES DID I EXCEL IN DURING THE PAST, SUCH AS IN MY CHILDHOOD/TEENAGE/COLLEGE YEARS?

exactly what you want to do with the components of your Soul Purpose; you want to put them in motion.

THE SOUL PURPOSE STAIRWAY

This model is intended to help you identify, simplify, and evaluate how to get on target! Elevate your Soul Purpose.

THE SOUL PURPOSE STAIRWAY
1. IMPLEMENTATION What one thing will you do immediately to start cultivating your Soul Purpose?
2. VALUE CREATION If you could only do one thing to earn an income what would it be?
3. CROSSOVER What one thing that you enjoy personally could also benefit you professionally?
4. RELATIONSHIPS Is there one relationship/situation in your life that drains your energy that could be immediately addressed, corrected, or eliminated?
5. AWARENESS If you could make only one improvement that would make a big difference in your life what would it be?

(Gunderson, Garrett. Soul Purpose Activator Guide, Freedom FastTrack Financial, *2011.)*

EATING OUR OWN COOKING

Froghair, the company I'm currently spending most of my time on, has spent a considerable amount of time wandering in the fog. As I explained in Chapter 1, when I started the company, it was a very low priority, we went through various permutations of ownership, it morphed into a little business I ran out of my garage with my boys, and I ultimately sold it. Then, when my partner and I bought Froghair back, we found that we needed to create a much clearer focus. Our beacon in the fog is now to become the leading agency in the outdoor sector that helps launch brands internationally. Our catalyzing statements have to do with specific benchmarks we have set for each month as we have tried to undo the damage created by the previous owner. And having those benchmarks (which will be discussed in more detail in subsequent chapters) has turned Froghair from a company that was under deep water financially into one that is beginning to make a profit and to move my partner and me toward our broader goals.

On a far more personal level, my overarching beacon in the fog is to make a dent in the poverty that permeates developing countries. But that is an overwhelming challenge, one that world leaders, philanthropic organizations, and development agencies have not been able to solve. Recognizing my inability to fix such an overwhelming issue with my limited means, I turned to a catalyzing statement that motivates me each day and has brought many like-minded individuals on board with me: to educate 1,000 young people from developing countries by the time I turn 50.

SUMMARY

The beacon in the fog is our destination. Where do we want to go? This is our big, audacious goal. For some, it is a dream vacation to France. For John F. Kennedy, it was having the best space program in the world. For me, it is educating young people in developing countries.

Our beacon in the fog is not a short-term goal; it is a long-term goal that our short-term goals are leading to. We then supplement it with our catalyzing statements, which add specificity. As we zigzag toward our individual beacons, it is essential that we pause long enough to climb high enough up a tree to see beyond the fog. We are then able to check our bearings to see if we are heading in the direction our zigzagging is supposed to be taking us.

Values—A Firm Foundation

Values are the infrastructure or highway system we travel on to reach our goal.

If my family and I were taking a road trip to Disneyland from our home in Utah, we would have two choices. We could pull out of our driveway, point our car southwest, and begin to drive through neighbors' dining rooms and yards, through cow pastures and weeds, across streams, and over mountain ranges until we got to sunny Southern California. The other choice would be to do an Internet search for the best route to Disneyland, and then print out and follow the directions that are given. I suppose option one would get us there eventually, if I had access to an amphibious assault vehicle—and if we could avoid arrest. But I think my family and I would enjoy the trip more if we followed the interstate—and exited the freeway once in a while for gas, a bite to eat, and a chance to freshen up.

Just as there are roads my family is willing to take and others we'd rather avoid, there are ways of living life and doing business that I am willing to try and others I steer clear of. For me, I love to drive on paved streets because I know my wife's minivan will get stuck in the mud if I head off across uncharted terrain. And, like a good map, my values keep me on the right roads.

Any organization that is going to be successful—whether it is a family, a sports team, or a business—must have a set of values to work from; otherwise, it will end up wandering into the weeds. When I say *values*, I'm not necessarily referring just to moral values. Values go well beyond what we may typically think of when we hear that word. They are the infrastructure you are going to use as you build toward your goal. Values include the behavior you are going to exhibit, the culture you want to create, and the rules you will follow. Values set the tone for what the culture in the company will be. Following or ignoring values creates the stories that then reinforce the culture we are building. Different families have different values, just as different businesses have different values. As an example, let's suppose you want to start a high-class restaurant with inventive food and a romantic environment. In this restaurant, you would value using fresh ingredients and having a meticulously clean kitchen. Quality, refinement, and culture might be some of the values you would promote among your staff and with your customers (whom you might refer to as patrons). On the other hand, if you were looking to open a family-friendly, fast-food restaurant, you would value speed, efficiency, variety, and the entertainment of kids. Ideally, you would value cleanliness as well. You are not going to use the same high-quality ingredients as your gourmet counterpart, and you might have far more options on the menu, including a kids' menu. Identifying your values, based on your purposes and objectives, is essential so you can clearly define where you're headed with your venture.

Although I do believe in right and wrong, it's important to initially assess your values without judgment. Different businesses must have different cultures and, therefore, values. A collections company that provides a service of calling people and demanding that they pay their bills will value employees who are assertive and who will not back down. The employees would generally value justice more than mercy. They would need to value responsibility and accountability. The employer might value being fair, but would define *fair* in terms of all the parties, with a bias toward the entity that is owed the money.

On the other hand, a company in the business of entertaining people would not flourish if it based its business on the same values as the collections agency. Typically, it would value fun, entertainment, preparation, and social interaction—those values that help ensure that everyone who walks in the door has fun.

It would not make sense for the entertainment company to say, "We are an entertainment company that is fair in our judgments." Likewise, you're not going to hear the collections agency say, "We value bringing joy and laughter to our patrons." Different businesses, different values.

I attended a very interesting lecture once where the speaker asked a group of chiropractors the following question: "Are you a healer? Are you a doctor? Or are you a businessperson?" There was a long and awkward pause, and then he continued, "Your response to this question is going to determine how you will set up and conduct your practice." The speaker wasn't suggesting there was a right or a wrong answer; he was saying that the answer would lead each of these chiropractors in a slightly different direction, so they ought to give it careful consideration.

Picture how the "healer" might set up his practice. He would be much more holistic in his approach, focusing on preventative care and wellness. In addition to his services, he might recommend and provide certain supplements and vitamins. He would likely encourage exercise and proper diets. He would certainly teach his patients proper techniques to avoid injury. His values would likely lead him to spend more time with each patient, which he'd need to consider as he mapped out his billing practices. He might spend more time with each customer and may or may not be as profitable.

The chiropractor who sees herself primarily as a doctor is likely more traditional and focuses on getting her patients' spines back into alignment. As such, her need for staff, office space, and billing policies are going to be quite different from the healer. Finally, the "businessperson" would have a dramatically different approach to his practice. He might not even do the day-to-day adjustments, opting instead to have a group of chiropractors work for him. He will be more focused on the production and efficiency of the practice. While these chiropractors' values may differ somewhat, what is clear is that their values are going to provide a road map that guides everything from selecting office space to determining rates to the actual care of the patients.

You can certainly head down the road not really knowing what your values are, but it's never going to get you anywhere good. For many years, my favorite college football team had an incredible coach. He was revered by fans, players, and coaches across the country. He coached the same team for almost three decades and won countless awards, including a national championship. He valued hiring great assistant coaches; and while there was no mistaking who was in charge, he was a delegator. When he took over his team as head coach, he could see it would never compete well with a running strategy, so he decided he would find quarterbacks who valued passing the ball. He faced teams that could score 20 or 30 points running the ball, but his team could score 40 or 50 by passing. So, they won. Several of his quarterbacks went on to play in the NFL, and more than one took his team to the Super Bowl.

He believed in his coaches, in his players, and in his strategy. On game day, he stood on the sidelines with his arms crossed, completely nonemotional as he calmly kept pace with his team from the sideline. If his team won, his expression was the same as those rare times that they lost.

After this coach retired, a coach came in who didn't seem to know what he valued. His offensive strategy seemed to change from week to week. He would start a quarterback, pull him out, and then try another quarterback. At times, he let his assistant coaches do their jobs, and other times he would take over—sometimes in the middle of a game. When a game was close, he would run up and down the sideline, waving his arms frantically over what was happening. Players and coaches alike didn't know what he expected of them; and, as a fan, it was confusing to watch the team during this time. No one seemed to know what he valued, and, as a result, it wasn't long before he was fired. Since leaving the university, he returned to the ranks of assistant coaches where he has had success, but no one has been willing to offer him a job as the head coach.

The most recent coach of this storied team is almost the exact opposite of the legendary coach. He is much more hands-on, to the point where he has functioned as both head coach and defensive coordinator. He is much more emotional. He is much more involved in the community, and expects his players to be as well. And yet, with all the differences, he is enjoying a winning record that rivals that of the man this school's football stadium is named after. The first coach and the current coach have succeeded with different values systems, but they each have one. And those values were and are crystal clear to each of the players and each member of the staff.

Whether you are deciding for yourself, your family, or your business, the values you settle on will determine your behavior, which will in turn determine what stories will be told about you. These stories will then serve to guide the behavior of those who follow you.

One of my heroes and mentors was a businessman named Ray Noorda. Ray was the CEO of Novell when I worked there, and he guided the company through its "glory days." During his time as CEO, everybody knew very clearly what the values of Novell were. Financial responsibility was at the top of the list. Next was to be on the leading edge of technology. Another was to take good care of customers.

We had a series of mantras that were propagated throughout the company. These were little statements that Ray was famous for, such as, "Resist change and die, adapt to change and survive, create change and thrive." Another was, "Customers first, employees second, shareholders third." One of his statements that used to spread fear throughout the company was, "Spring cleaning whether we need it or not." All of us knew that every spring the bottom 10 percent of performers would be laid off. Ray did not like having dead wood in the company. He felt it was an honor to work at Novell; and if people were not performing, he did not want them to weigh the company down. Not everyone agreed with his values, but these are examples of the culture that Ray created for Novell.

Most of us who worked for Ray considered him to be something of a tightwad. Whether that is a fair assessment or not, he was definitely fiscally responsible. Although he was a billionaire, Ray did not have a fancy office; in fact, he had the same standard issue desk and chairs as everyone else. When he traveled, he flew coach to save the company money. He did not wear expensive suits. He drove an old 1972 King Cab pickup truck.

Not surprisingly, he loved to walk around the company and meet people. He would stay after hours and talk with the custodians. It was not uncommon for him to come sit on your desk and ask if you had anything good to eat. He would talk to every level of employee. As a result, he knew exactly what was happening in the company.

At one point, we had an executive who made it a point to let others know he had money, and one day he came to work with a shiny new Rolex watch. This employee had failed to take note of the values and culture of the company. Not surprisingly, he was one of those who ended up getting cleaned out the next spring. That became one of the many stories that got passed through the company, which reinforced the values Ray used to guide Novell.

One time I personally witnessed one of Ray's stories, and I did my part to pass it along. I was in the restroom when Ray walked in. There was another man in there who was combing his hair and who kept the water on the entire time he was grooming himself. He would leave the water running while he went to check himself in the mirror. Then he'd come back for a bit more water, and then head to the mirror again. When Ray came in and saw what was going on, he turned the water off. The guy went back and turned it back on—and then gave Ray a dirty look. As the guy turned away from the water, Ray shut it off again. It was obvious this guy had no idea who he was dealing with. After the third time, Ray wagged his finger in this man's face and said, "Waste not, want not." I am not sure what happened to the offender. But I know that I was sure quivering and that the value of not being wasteful was ingrained deep within me that day. These were the stories that would spread like wildfire through the company. They taught the values and created the culture of how everyone in the company was expected to behave.

Values Will Guide Us
through the Rough Times

I know of a mother who had a lot of children. In fact, some people looked down on her for having so many, but she didn't care. She loved her children. She had very little materially, but she would look at her kids and say, "I will put you up there with the best of them." She had a big goal out there. It was not only to raise good kids: she wanted to raise children who would be hardworking and self-reliant. She wanted her kids to go out and make a difference in the world. This was her beacon in the fog.

This family did not have many resources. They lived on a dairy farm at a time when milk prices were dropping. The entire time this family was being raised, there was not one year that their total income was above the poverty level; in fact, many years it was well below the poverty level. But this inconvenience did not deter this mother. She had a set of values she was determined to pass along to her children, and those values guided everything she did. Some of the things she valued were education, hard work, and self-reliance. She did not want her kids to be dependent on society like many other families in their situation.

This mother got creative with the meager resources she had, and she taught her children that if there was something they wanted, they needed to do the same. One of her daughters wanted to take dance lessons like the other girls in her class. This mother talked with the dance teacher; and even though the mother did not have cash to pay for the lessons, the dance teacher happily took milk and eggs from her farm in exchange for those lessons. Another child needed some expensive dental care. The mother went to work at a dental office in exchange for the needed treatment. This family was growing up in the 1970s and '80s before personal computers were common. As her kids became teenagers, the mother would encourage them to take typing classes so they could get a good after-school job. She then allowed the kids to be responsible for their own expenses and learn how to manage their money. As busy as she was and as much as she stressed self-reliance, she always encouraged them in their homework and helped them seek out scholarships.

Once, one of her children was noticing all the name-brand clothes her peers were wearing. She stopped the mother and asked, "Mom, are we poor?" The mother thought for a minute or two and replied, "No, we are not poor; we are just broke." She wanted her daughter to realize that even though they did not have a lot of money at the time, they could work hard and move up to become whatever they wanted to be. In her mind a "poor" person was someone with a victim mentality, and she did not want her children to feel as though life was just owed to them.

Another time one of the daughters wanted to try out for the cheerleading squad. Both the mother and the daughter knew the uniforms, shoes, trips, and fees cost a lot of money. So they brainstormed together about how to make this work. The daughter got a summer job moving sprinklers and working at Kentucky Fried Chicken to pay for the things she needed. She had to work a little harder than the other girls on the squad, but those things made her strong.

In the end, every one of this mother's children went to college and then on to productive careers. Each one of these children is contributing to society in his and her chosen field. One is a doctor, another an engineer. There is a nurse, a businessman, a businesswomen, and a teacher. Now that her children are grown, people say to this mom "You are so lucky. How did you do it?" She smiles, knowing it had nothing to do with luck.

She had established her goals and values before she even had children. And those children were clearly shown the road map they should follow if they wanted to achieve success.

VALUES ARE NOT ALWAYS CONVENIENT

During the 2010–2011 basketball season, a college basketball team that had fielded a lot of good teams over the years had a great team. Led by a young man who was the nation's leading scorer and who smashed school records that had stood for 30 years, this team moved into the top five in national rankings. As the NCAA tournament approached, fans and pundits alike saw the team as a strong contender for making it to the Elite Eight, the Final Four, and maybe even beyond. Then, not even two weeks before the NCAA tournament was set to begin, perhaps the second-best player on the team was suddenly suspended. Why? Well, the details are his business, but it was clear he had violated his school's honor code—a set of values every student had agreed to live by, athlete or not. The violation was such that he was allowed to remain in school, but he was not allowed to play.

Not surprisingly, the team lost its next game. It regrouped and won the final game of the season, and then lost the final game of the conference tournament. Where it had only lost two games all season, in a week's time it had lost four! And when the NCAA invites came out, this team slipped from a lock on a number-one seed to a number-three seed.

Of course, there was a lot of talk about this young man's suspension. Some wondered why the school felt a need to stick to its values when so much was on the line. Each time the team played without this young man, it was evident that, while it was still good, the team had lost its chance at greatness. And, indeed, it lost in the Sweet Sixteen.

What it didn't lose was its commitment to its values. The school had a clearly stated policy on which behaviors were acceptable and which ones weren't, and it stuck by them in an age when expediency often takes the place of integrity. Some people felt the school had made a tough call. And while it likely was a painful decision for administrators to make, it really wasn't a tough call—it was an outgrowth of values that, for years, had been clearly delineated and adhered to.

As a footnote, this young man held his head high, he didn't complain, he even continued to sit with his team in shirt and tie and cheer them on. And when he climbed up the ladder to help cut down the net after the final home game (just four days after his suspension), he was greeted with a standing ovation from a crowd of 21,000 fans. And while I can't predict the future, most feel he will serve out his suspension and return to the team for the 2011–2012 season.

MAKING OUR VALUES CLEAR

When our children were young, we made a family mission statement. Mission statements are a little antiquated now, but my wife and I wanted to define the values that we wanted to live by in our family. Some of the values we listed were:

⇨ Our family will support each other in our goals and ambitions.

⇨ Our home will be an environment of safety, love, and respect.

⇨ We will provide unconditional love for each other.

⇨ We will teach respect for people, places, and things.

⇨ We will embrace the value of hard work and leadership.

⇨ We will allow each other to make mistakes and grow from these mistakes, but we will encourage each other to reach for higher levels.

⇨ We will have positive friendships.

⇨ Our family will work together, play together, and stay together.

⇨ We will laugh often and savor the good, while fearlessly fighting the bad.

⇨ We will act on life and turn negative situations into positives.

⇨ We will value learning and education.

⇨ Each family member will strive to make a meaningful contribution to humanity.

Our family is far from perfect, but these are some of the values we set out to teach our children. We have the list posted in our entryway, and each member of our family knows what is expected of them. And I'm always amused at the stories our children tell each other and their friends of the funny things that happen in our family as we reinforce these values.

Rick Sapio talks about what he calls "value-based decision making." He also refers to "The Doorman Principle," which is defined as "the deliberate practice of defining a set of values and/ or rules to dictate who, or what, is allowed to enter into your life or business." In our lives and in our businesses, we must have a "value gatekeeper." In our home, my wife is the value gate-keeper. When she sees one of my sons being rude to his friends, she will call him on it because, "We teach respect for people, places, and things." She insists that our kids do their homework because, "We value education." She does not let riffraff into our home and encourages our children to have positive friendships.

Koral, my executive administrator, is the "value gate-keeper" at my office. She keeps the distractions and business snakes out of my life. Koral is responsible for the final inter-view of every potential hire. She deliberately does an exhaus-tive interview to ensure the person is in alignment with the 12 values of our organization. If the candidate does not pass this check, they do not get hired no matter how talented they are.

VALUES EXERCISE

A powerful and valuable exercise that I like to use is from Rick Sapio.

1. Write down three people in your life that you most admire or respect and who you most want to be like.

2. From the values assessment lists on pages 75 and 76, circle seven or eight values that best describe each of those people.

3. Those values that show up repeatedly will be the things that you value.

This simple exercise will bring great clarity to what your values are. From my experience, you will end up with about 10 values with which you closely align yourself.

After you have established your values, do not let anyone into your intimate circle that does not fit with your values. Of course, it's naive to think that you will never have to deal with anyone who doesn't share exactly the same values, but I'm talking about your inside circle or trust relationships. That means your important hires, your friends, your partnerships. You need to establish a value gatekeeper that you have complete trust in to make sure that your values are honored. These values help you surround yourself with people who align closely with you.

Each company or organization needs to make its own set of values and rules that it wants to live by. Rick has a few rules based on his values that determine the kinds of people he will hire. Some examples of these rules include:

1. They must be responsible.

2. They must have a credit score about 700.

VALUE ASSESSMENT

Achievement/Drive	Ecological Awareness
Adaptability	Economic Security
Adding Value	Effectiveness
Advancement and Promotion	Efficiency
Adventure	Ethical Practice
Aesthetic	Empathy
Affection (love and caring)	Endurance
Affinity	Energy
Aliveness	Enthusiasm
Arts	Environment
Attractiveness	Equality
Authenticity	Excellence
Awareness	Excitement
Beauty	Expertise
Bliss	Expression
Caring	Fairness
Certainty	Fame
Challenging Problems	Family
Change and Variety	Fast Living
Charisma	Fast-Paced Work
Charity	Financial Gain
Cheerfulness	Flexibility
Chivalry	Focus
Clarity	Forgiveness
Close Relationships	Freedom
Coaching	Friendship
Commitment	Fun
Communication	Giving
Companionship	Gratitude
Compassion	Growth
Competence	God
Competition	Happiness
Confidence	Having a Family
Congruence	Health
Connection	Heart
Conscientiousness	Helping Other People
Considerate	Helping Society
Contribution	Honesty
Conviction	Honor
Cooperation	Inclusive
Courage	Independence
Courteousness	Influencing Others
Creativity	Inner Harmony
Decisiveness	Inspiration
Democracy	Integrity
Dependability	Intellectual Status
Discernment	Intelligence
Discovery	Intention

VALUE ASSESSMENT	Page 2

Intimacy	Rational
Involvement	Receptivity
Job Tranquility	Recognition
Joy	(respect from others, status)
Justice	Reliability
Kindness	Religion
Knowledge	Reputation
Leadership	Resolution
Learning	Resolve
Leverage	Resourcefulness
Life	Respect
Location	Responsibility and Accountability
Love	Security
Loyalty	Self-Determinism
Making a difference	Self-Respect
Market Position	Sensitivity
Meaningful Work	Sensuality
Mentorship	Serenity
Meditation	Sharing
Merit	Simplicity
Money/Making Money	Sophistication
Music	Soul
Nature	Spirit
Nurturing	Spiritual
Open and Honest	Spontaneity
(i.e. being around people who are)	Stability
Openness	Strength
Partnership	Status
Passion	Success
Patience	Supervising Others
Peace	Synergy
Perception	Team/Teamwork
Perseverance	Technology
Personal Growth & Development	Tenderness
(living up to the fullest potential)	Time Freedom
Physical Challenge	Togetherness
Playfulness	Travel
Pleasure	Trust
Power and Authority	Trustworthiness
Presence	Truth
Privacy	Unity
Probability	Value
Productivity	Vigor
Public Service	Vision
Purity	Vitality
Purpose	Vulnerability
Quality	Wealth
Quality Relationships	Wisdom

3. They must have a college degree.

4. They must have a minimum of five years' experience in their profession.

Some of his rules for the people that he won't hire are:

1. He will not hire anyone who is a close friend.

2. He will not hire anyone who has been unemployed for a long period of time.

3. He will not hire anyone who does not value what we value.

4. He will not hire anyone who is late to an interview.

Listing the values that you want to travel on in your organization is not just limited to your business. You should set up values and rules to travel on in other areas of your life where you are striving to reach a goal. Some of these areas could include:

⇨ Projects that you are involved in

⇨ Charitable groups you are involved with

⇨ Organizations that your children are involved in

⇨ Your children's friends

⇨ Future business decisions

⇨ Your personal habits

⇨ Your health and well-being

These are some of the ideas that Rick came up with, but this list should be personally tailored to you, your essential nature, your hopes and dreams, and your abilities. Using value-based decision making can help you in your business, key relationships, parenting efforts, and virtually every other area of your life. These values will help you avoid mistakes and make you more aware of where you are traveling on this road to success.

EATING OUR OWN COOKING

As soon as we realized that we were getting our trading company back, Curtis and I sat down and mapped out the values we felt were essential for Froghair. We went through the values assessment exercises and came up with the following list:

⇨ **Competence**. We are a competent team.

⇨ **Cooperation**. We value teamwork. We work together, we win together, and we waddle together. We cooperate.

⇨ **Freedom**. We believe in freedom—not only for the company but also in our personal lives. We support and help our team members to become free—financially, physically, and mentally free.

⇨ **Helping society**. We believe in helping society. There are a lot of human needs. The most important is to live, love, learn, and matter. We want to give back and to make a difference.

⇨ **Independence**. We believe in being accountable for our own destiny. We're not big believers in grants and hand-outs. We take accountability for our own destiny.

⇨ **Integrity**. We try to do the right thing. We are not always perfect, but our intent is to consciously work toward doing the right thing.

⇨ **Leadership**. Leadership can be lonely, but we have the courage to stand out in the cold if need be to do the right things, even if those things are not popular.

⇨ **Responsibility and accountability**. We have an attitude of "I'll do it!" We don't say, "I'll try to get around to it"; we just do it. Not only do we do it, we take accountability for what happens—good or bad.

⇨ **Gratitude**. We're a company of gratitude. We're grateful to God. We're grateful to each other. We're grateful for our relationships and for the opportunities we have. We expect our team members to be grateful as well.

⇨ **Culturally sensitive**. We embrace the people and places of the world. We value diversity. We work on a daily basis with a wide variety of ethnic and religious groups, without bias.

These are the values we have worked hard to establish. Our infrastructure is solidly in place, and it helps us ensure that we bring people into the culture of our company who are in alignment with our values.

SUMMARY

These first three chapters have set the foundation for us to deliberately begin to zig and zag. You first assessed all of your resources so that you know what you are starting with, at your beginning point. Then you defined your beacon in the fog, or your destination point. You know where you are going. You have passion and a catalyzing statement that is the emotional fuel that will propel your vehicle to your destination. Finally, you have defined the values or road system that you will take to get you to your final goal. These four elements are what will get you on your way to your first zig! In the next chapter we'll be tackling zig number 1—driving to profitability.

Zig Number 1—Drive to Profitability

As children leave the comforts of home for the first time, they typically fall into one of two categories. There are those who, having grown accustomed to a nice house, an abundance of food, and easy access to a car, feel they should enjoy this same lifestyle now that they are out on their own. If their solution is to max out credit cards and run up student loans, then what happens? They get partway to their destination—whether that's schooling or building a career—and run out of resources. Then there are those who ration what little they have, avoid borrowing at every turn, and wait until they're firmly established before trying to live the same life it took their parents years to build.

As I share my ideas on focusing your first zig down the hill on your drive to profitability, I know some readers are going to feel I'm placing an undue emphasis on business principles. And while I probably am, in part because that's the world I live in, I also want to point out that the principle of driving toward profitability has application in all aspects of our lives, whether we're bootstrapping a business, building a family, or overseeing a multimillion-dollar enterprise. In fact, I would contend that this first zig of getting to profitability is important in every aspect of our lives because while it's true that money can't buy happiness, being broke can sure cause a lot of headaches.

When my wife and I first got married, we were both in school and broke, and I had to take several jobs I wasn't all that excited about. I even had to work late-night shifts when I would have preferred being home because I instinctively knew I needed to do whatever it took to get to profitability. Neither of us had come from an abundance of wealth, but during our early years we tightened our budget and were so conservative that the humble origins we had grown up in looked like the lifestyle of the rich and famous. So, we drove that old Dodge Colt that had been given to me, even though I'm sure we could have qualified for a loan to buy a new car.

We had enough resources to pay our bills, even though our $15-per-week food budget did require that we eat a lot of potatoes during those times. My wife reminds me that I used to always say, "We will live like you won't now, so we can live like you can't later." At that stage of my life, I hadn't given words to the idea of driving to profitability, but I knew instinctively the importance of that principle.

Whether you are starting out in life or starting a business—or are broke and starting over—your first zig always needs to take you toward profitability. Profitability means you're able to pay all of your bills and have enough cash to move forward with your plans. Given the ease of finding money, whether it's from a credit card, a government grant, a small business loan, or help from family, it's easy to bypass this first step. But at some point the wells of easy cash will dry up, and you'll find yourself at a day of reckoning where if you don't have real cash coming in, you're going to be stopped dead in your tracks. So, don't let the easy allure of available cash sidetrack you from finding the path that will get you to that critical point of profitability.

This first zig requires sheer grit and raw determination. I often joke that when I am starting a new business I will go out in the street and dance in a tutu if that is what it takes to get to profitability. And while my efforts have never come to that, I will do what it takes, within the framework of my values, to get enough cash to move forward. Operating from the black gives you a much higher level of confidence and a sense of durability that you can't have if you're always worrying about draining your bank account. If you have money in the bank or cash in your pocket, you can breathe a sigh of relief as you keep trying different things until you get one of your ideas to work. And if you can't get an idea to be profitable, then check it off your list and try something different. (This is what I call failing efficiently, which we'll discuss in more detail later in the chapter.)

Just before the dot.com bubble burst in the early 2000s, I was working as the general manager of a company called MyJobSearch.com. It was a heavily funded business in the web 1.0 Internet bubble phase. This was a wild and crazy time when companies were being built and funded by people writing business plans on paper napkins. This company had hired 40 or 50 employees, and we didn't even know what the exact product was that we were building. And, because we were living on investment bankers, we had no clue how we were ever going to get to profitability. Heck, we didn't need to!

When the bubble burst, everything imploded. Not just for this company but for almost every other company in the web industry. The reason this company and those other companies failed was because they were not built for profitability. We had never needed to pursue that strategy. In fact, during this time, the strategy for most of these companies was to get an IPO and then get bought up by a bigger company. But, as countless people who lost huge sums of money found out, that is not a business plan that can be sustained.

So many businesses I've seen think that all they have to do is head straight for that beacon in the fog. It doesn't work. The first zig always needs to be to get cash!

FINDING HIDDEN ASSETS

When I am starting a business, the first question I ask myself is, "What skills do I have that can get me to profitability the fastest?" (And this same question should be asked whether we're trying to build a business or any other part of our life.) The answer doesn't have to be perfectly aligned with your beacon in the fog, just something that is close enough and is an inch or two up from where you currently are. (Remember, we're zigzagging.) While I was in college majoring in electronic engineering, I found a job at a computer repair shop. It certainly wasn't where I wanted to end up, but I was able to get cash for my family and also learn skills that would bring me closer to my goal of graduating in engineering.

When my partner, Ron Porter, and I started CastleWave, I had a knack (for which I had been well paid) for getting key words to the top of the search engines on the Internet. I had sworn I would not share any of my search engine optimization (SEO) secrets and mental knowledge with other people because I was done making other people rich and I was in the mode of creating my own businesses. But in the earliest days of CastleWave, I realized that the fastest way to cash was to fill the need other companies had for SEO work.

I had some contacts in New York City who I knew wanted to get their own websites to the top of the search engines. So Ron and I flew to New York and sold these contacts on search engine optimization. We were almost instantly profitable because I was willing to do what I regarded as the equivalent of going out in the street and dancing in a tutu. I did not initially do what I wanted to do; instead, I zigged to the fastest source of cash I could identify because I understood how important that first zig is.

MINIMIZE YOUR RISKS

I once worked with some individuals who operated a very successful insurance practice. They had a great business financially, but they were utterly uninspired by what they were doing. They were not moving toward their beacon in the fog in any part of their life, and they were frustrated—not to mention running on fumes. At the same time, they had a great idea for a very progressive technology. That was where their true passion was. They knew they had something good and had even started filing the patent for their idea.

The problem was that every time they started down the path and began to make some progress, they would shift into panic mode. I could actually see the anxiety and pressure building up in their faces and their eyes. As I did some digging to understand what was holding them back, I finally was able to find out what was going on. They were worried their business model might not work. They would get partway down the path and then just freeze. They were afraid of failure. They knew so many entrepreneurs who had done the equivalent of running to Vegas and putting everything on black—and most of the time they had failed. Then they would head home broke and deal with lives that had been ruined.

When I finally understood what was holding them back, I said, "Listen, you don't have to bet the farm. You don't have to give away your soul. You don't have to risk everything you value and believe in to succeed as an entrepreneur. There is a better way. It's okay to use your insurance business as a base and then zigzag to success." I then outlined the steps they should take. It was as if someone had pulled a huge, sopping wet blanket off of them. They got so excited. The fear left their eyes and their faces lit up. And soon they were zigzagging toward their beacon in the fog.

THE NEED FOR PACING

From my own experiences, I have found that when people set their beacon in the fog and then head directly toward it without zigzagging, one of three things will occur:

1. They never do it. There are lots of people who talk and talk about their dream and what they are going to do; but then, before they've taken their first step, their knees shake and wobble, and they don't dare take the risk

needed to progress toward their goal. I used to think these people were just weak-hearted, but I've decided that subconsciously they realize there is a chance they may fail so they do not even start.

2. The second group of people race toward their goal full speed ahead, and when they get halfway there, they run out of resources and fail.

3. The third group runs straight toward their goal, but by the time they get there, the target has completely moved and their great idea is now a lost opportunity. In many cases, if they had taken their blinders off and looked from side to side occasionally, they would have seen the need to adjust their course.

Zigzagging deliberately toward your goal makes the going slower. It is more methodical and might seem harder, especially for those of us who lack patience. But there is a much higher chance of success because zigzagging allows you to inch toward your goal and then adjust and adapt until you actually get to viability.

One of the benefits of this approach is that it puts you in a mindset of abundance by setting parameters for what you can and can't risk or lose. And when that happens, you find yourself free from the fear of scarcity, which tends to paralyze us rather than motivate us. An example of this approach is found in the success story of the Marriott Corporation. In the 1920s, J. Willard Marriott opened a nine-stool A&W Root Beer stand in Washington DC. As time went on he realized that people bought lots of root beer in the hot summer months but not so much during winter. So he started selling soup as well and changed the name to The Hot Shoppe. In the early days, he and his partners worked lots of long hours to get their shop to profitability. As they looked for additional opportunities, they obtained the food service management contract with the U.S. Department of Treasury. Then during World War II, The Hot Shoppe catered to the many defense people who moved to the nation's capital.

It wasn't until 1957 that Bill Marriott opened his first hotel. As the business grew, he found parallel opportunities as his company grew into one of the largest hotel chains in the world. Some of those ventures included expanding the food business to service major airlines and buying additional restaurants like Bob's Big Boy. With each new project, Bill was able to get enough cash to move on to his bigger goals (www.marriott.com/careers/history). This is a great example of a company starting small and zigzagging its way up to long-term strength and success.

Many first businesses revolve around services. The reason is that service businesses can usually get you to cash quickly. The downside is that they are often labor intensive in the beginning. At the early stage, you are literally the butcher, the baker, and the candlestick maker all rolled into one because you typically don't have any (or many) employees, and so you have to carry the brunt of the work.

For example, when we started CastleWave, Ron and I had to be the salespeople to land our first account in New York.

I then had to be the programmer and had to personally optimize the website. We also had to be the secretary and bookkeeper and take care of billing and collecting the money. This was very time-consuming work, but it did bring in the first bursts of cash that allowed CastleWave to get off the ground.

GETTING IDEAS FOR YOUR FIRST ZIG

The question that is asked of me as an entrepreneur more than any other question is: "Hey, I've got this really cool idea. What do you think? Is this viable? Will it get me to cash?" Coming up with an idea is the easy part. The harder part is figuring out what is a good idea and what is a bad idea. One of the first resources I use when I am vetting ideas is my modified version of a "Porter Model" based on Michael E. Porter's Five Forces Competitive Position Model (Michael E. Porter,

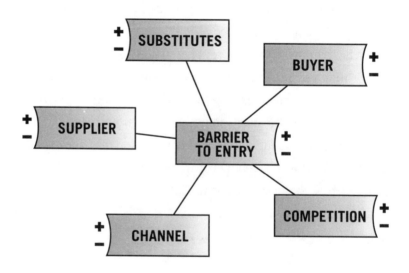

Competitive Strategy: Techniques for Analyzing Industries and Competitors. New York: Free Press, 1998).

In my model there are six factors to look at. These are:

1. Barrier to Entry

    a. How difficult is it to enter this market space?

    b. Do you have an advantage over the competition?

    c. Once in, how do you keep others out of the space?

2. Supplier

    a. How much power do you have over the suppliers?

    b. Are there multiple suppliers available?

    c. Can you get a better price on your supplies than the competition?

3. Substitutes

    a. Is there a feature of your product or service that would compel customers to buy your product over the competitions'?

    b. Is there a substitute that will compete with your product?

4. Buyer

    a. What is the bargaining power of the buyers? Do your target buyers have the power to force the price of your product down?

    b. Can you command a premium price for your product?

5. Competition

    a.   Who is competing for market share in your product? Is the market saturated?

    b.   Is there a rivalry among competitors in the industry? Note that competition can be a good thing unless it squashes your chances of entering the market.

6. Channel

    a.   Do you have access to a distribution channel? Channel is probably the most important of all the factors. If there is not a market need for your product and a way to get it to the customer, then your business will fail. In the businesses I create, I will not move forward until I have fully figured out the channel. Most people think they will build the product, then try to sell it. The correct order is to ensure that the market will buy your product, then determine how you will deliver it to your customers and only then go ahead a build it.

    b.   Do you know who is going to buy your product or service?

For each factor, you will come up with several questions similar to what I have posed above. The answer to each question will receive a positive (+), a negative (–), or a neutral (0) result, ending in a final overall score for each factor. As you look at the positives and negatives of your business idea, you will be able to see rather clearly if it is an idea that will work or just a pipe dream.

As you look for ideas, there are a couple of things you should remember to avoid. The first is what I refer to as "the rabbit syndrome." Some people see ideas popping out everywhere they look. They'll spot a great idea or concept and proclaim, "Look! A rabbit!" Then they see another and another and another (if you've spent any time in rabbit country, you know they're everywhere). They chase one rabbit after another and end up so busy chasing every rabbit that pops up that they never actually drive to profitability. At some point you have to settle on *one* rabbit and chase it as hard as your can—hopefully to the successful end.

Another mistake you want to avoid is falling in love with an idea to the point where you can't see its deficiencies.

In 1989 I contributed my fair share to making my first $2 million business mistake. I keep the box pictured below on my life-trophy shelf to remind me never to make this mistake again.

So what was it we made?

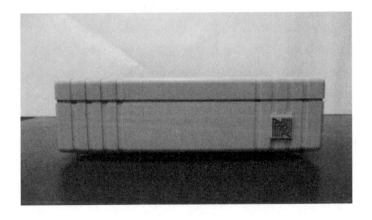

We did what so many eager engineering types do—we built a way cool, exciting, leading-edge product (in this case, a digital power line transmission device) and then tried to sell it.

In our engineering minds, we just knew customers would buy these boxes by the truckloads. We had attended the trade shows and been mobbed by fellow engineers who thought our idea was awesome, which convinced us this product was going to be a barn burner. Everyone told us we were so smart and this was the cooooooolest technology ever.

Well, cool technology does not necessarily lead to actual customers, and in 1990 the company went belly up! Why? Because our product did exactly what a $20 power cable could do, only our box cost $995 apiece. And, in our zeal, we engineers never stopped to consider that, if given the choice, people would opt for the $20 cable, even though our technology was "better."

And, lest you think engineers are the only ones who get too focused on their great ideas, I have an associate who has a fervent desire to promote ultra-modern cement homes. He has wanted to create a business around these buildings because he is passionate about the benefits they provide. Indeed the concept and these homes are amazing. The only problem is that he lives in a community where the homes are built using wood, bricks, stucco, and traditional architecture. In spite of his efforts, the people in his community have not caught on to his vision of building cement homes. You do not want to create a product in which consumers have no interest because if you don't have a channel to sell your products through, your business will fail.

How Much Cash Do I Need?

I define profitability as having enough money to cover "the nut" and having a buffer that will allow me to move on to the next zag. Everyone has different needs, or "nuts," so profitability will be different for each person or each business. I am covering the nut in my personal life when I have enough money to pay all my expenses, such as housing, utilities, recreation, food, clothing, education needs, health insurance, and a little more to take care of those unexpected extras that always crop up.

If a family makes a budget and keeps track of how much it costs to live each month, then that is the family's monthly nut. In business, the nut would include the building, utilities, the cost of doing business, payroll for any employees, and any other expenses it takes to run the business, including paying yourself. (If you forget that, you'll destroy the nut in your personal life.) Use the worksheet on page 96 as a guide to determining your nut. Any amount over these expenses is profit. You need to carefully calculate what it's going to cost you to get to profitability. This can't be a number you guess at. It needs to be a firm number and one that you write down. Here is some help in coming up with that number.

Components of Zig Number 1

Because your first zig is so important, I want to dissect its components and look at each one individually next.

FIGURE YOUR NUT (SAMPLE)

What number do you have to make per month to hit profitability?

GROSS REVENUE (How much money you bring in per month) $ 20,000.00

EXPENSES Rent $ 1,000.00
          Utilities $ 500.00
          Payroll $ 5,000.00
          Office Supplies $ 200.00
          Travel $ 500.00
          Guaranteed Payment to Self $ 5,000.00
          Legal and Professional Fees $ 200.00
          Phones $ 800.00
          Insurance $ 1,000.00
          Misc. $ 500.00

TOTAL EXPENSES (Your Nut) $ 14,700.00

NET INCOME (Gross Revenue Minus Total Expenses) $ 5,300.00

FIGURE YOUR NUT

GROSS REVENUE (How much money you bring in per month) $_____

EXPENSES _____ $_____
          _____ $_____
          _____ $_____
          _____ $_____
          _____ $_____
          _____ $_____
          _____ $_____
          _____ $_____
          _____ $_____
          _____ $_____

TOTAL EXPENSES (Your Nut) $_____

NET INCOME (Gross Revenue Minus Total Expenses) $_____

FINANCIAL NUMBER

Zig number 1 is a financial number. You have to have a financial target number specifying how much you want to bring in. Refer back to the nut you determined in the last section.

ALLOCATION OF TIME

How much time are you going to dedicate to getting to cash? How long will you give yourself to achieve this financial target? I will typically dedicate 65 percent of my resources toward getting to profitability, 30 percent toward zag number 2, and 5 percent toward zig number 3. And, as I look ahead, I never plan beyond three zigzags.

DURATION OF TIME

How long are you willing to run at this pace? Anyone can sprint for a block or two. But what reserves do you have if you end up needing to run a marathon?

FINANCIAL TARGET

What is your target for the profit you want to make? How and why is this different from the financial number above? After you have covered the nut, what is your goal for how much profit you want to make?

FINANCIAL RESOURCES

How much in the way of financial resources are you willing to invest? How do you want to allocate *your* financial resources? In the early days of entrepreneurship, I used to be more willing to mortgage my house or use my emergency buffer to help fund my businesses. Now I have a policy: I absolutely will not mortgage my house or dip into my safety net. We will talk more about this in Chapter 7 when we talk about guardrails.

RELATIONSHIP CAPITAL

We have already talked about relationship capital in Chapter 1. Think carefully about how much relationship capital you want to use when driving to profitability. One of the reasons I choose not to sell to my close family and friends is because I am not willing to expend all my relationship capital in one fell swoop. It is important in the early stages of your business not to drain your whole relationship bank account. Selectively choose a few key individuals who can help you, but carefully define and limit how much relationship capital you're willing to spend. Then make sure you give those people a "thank you" and put something back into their relationship bank account. Gratitude goes a long way with relationship capital.

GIVE YOURSELF PERMISSION TO BE MISERABLE

I'll be honest; this is not an easy stage. Sometimes, in getting to cash, I have to do a lot of things I really don't like doing. I have to do the books, answer the phone calls, and open the mail. I do it all! I can do it; I just don't like to do it. So I give myself permission to be miserable and endure—but only for so long.

RESOURCE LIST

To help you quantify your responses to these questions, here's a worksheet on the next page that will help you see in black and white the road you're considering heading down. Use the results from your Value Equation on page 30 to help populate this worksheet.

THE 80/20 RULE

During this first zig, it is important to remember that you are not going to have time to be perfect at everything. Many people who are perfectionists or have a methodical personality type fail at this stage because they try to be great and

99

RESOURCE LIST
1. HOW MUCH MONEY DO YOU HAVE TO PUT TOWARD THIS PROJECT? $ _____
2. HOW MUCH TIME EACH WEEK ARE YOU ABLE OR WILLING TO DEDICATE TO THIS PROJECT? _____ hours
3. HOW LONG OF A TIMEFRAME DO YOU HAVE TO WORK WITH? _____ months/years
4. EMOTIONALLY, HOW LONG CAN YOU GIVE YOURSELF TO ACCOMPLISH THIS GOAL? _____ months/years
5. HOW MUCH PAIN (EMOTIONAL, FINANCIAL, RELATIONSHIP, TIME) ARE YOU WILLING TO ENDURE?

have everything perfect and buttoned up. You need to think, instead, about the 80/20 rule. In general, 20 percent of the effort yields 80 percent of the results. The key to success is not to do anything that isn't geared toward the 80 percent success ratio. You're not striving for perfection. You're striving for profitability.

I always say that competence and incompetence rear their heads. But it is important during this time to know those things where competency is a must. If you produce a shoddy product, then your customers will never use you again. But, as you do so, you do not need the perfect organization or to micromanage all the details. During this phase the important 20 percent is providing a quality product and getting to cash.

If your office is a mess or you haven't taken the trash out in a week, take a deep breath and give yourself a break. You can get to those things later.

On the other hand, it is imperative that you keep track of your books and know what your bottom line is, but don't stress about the little things as you take care of the big ones. I have a former business associate who had the mantra on his desk to "Strive for Mediocrity." He was a perfectionist in every area of his life. If he saw a "t" that needed to be crossed or an "i" that needed to be dotted, he would take whatever time it took to stress over minor details. He soon found he could not be effective living this way. He had to look at the bigger picture and choose which things he needed to focus on to succeed, and then let go of the minor things. He was trying to be more "mediocre" in the smaller details so that he could shine in the important aspects of the business. One of my business partners used to call this "selective negligence." He would selectively neglect the less important things so that he could achieve the bigger goals. Once we became profitable and got to the next zag of adding resources, we could hire someone to take care of those small details.

This can be applied whether you are an individual trying to accomplish an important project with your family, a small bootstrap company, or a large corporation. You can apply this same principle to a new division you may be heading up or to a new product or a new service you may be launching in a large corporation. Your budget may be bigger, but the principles will make the division or large corporation even stronger.

Fail Efficiently

I've learned a great deal over the years about failing efficiently. When I use the word "fail," I'm not talking about falling off tall buildings, going bankrupt, or losing everything. What I mean by failing efficiently is that if you can't get to profitability, you need to accept that you have nowhere left to go. You have to become financially profitable before you go on to the next step. I see far too many people say, "Oh, well, if I just add resources and scale, *then* I'll get to profitability!" But they are inevitably wrong.

Failing efficiently means that unless you hit profitability in whatever time you've allocated, you are done! You need to stop. If you do, you've failed efficiently and life goes on. If you aren't willing to stop, you will fail at a level that may have devastating consequences.

In your personal life, if you keep going into debt without getting to profitability, you will end up in financial ruin. You cannot keep trying to add resources or buy more and more things unless you have the cash to pay for them. (And while, yes, credit can be easy to get, at some point you'll max out and no one will loan you more money.) Become profitable in your life, in whatever pursuit you have undertaken.

Eating Our Own Cooking

When we took back Froghair, we decided that Curtis would not quit his full-time job to come on board until we had $60,000 in the bank as a buffer. We felt that a three-month buffer was a safety net we would be comfortable with and that it would take the pressure off in case we had any kind of a hiccup.

To begin with, we were working Froghair as a fifth priority. I was taking time off to hike in the Himalayas after selling CastleWave, and Curtis had other priorities. We had a part-time college student named Shane who was helping us. In August 2010, we sat down and defined our zig number 1. After looking at our expenses, we determined and wrote down our financial target number, which was that we needed to net $25,000 a month in order to be profitable. We were both dedicated to putting 65 percent of our resources toward this effort.

Other than Shane, we did not hire any employees until we hit this target, so the three of us were doing everything. We had a lot of motivation to reach our goal of becoming profitable before January 1, 2011. We also set a goal to have five new, high-profile brands in place. On December 1, 2010, we officially hit this goal one month ahead of schedule. In November we posted $382,600 of sales with $51,195 in net profit. Now, having hit that target, we celebrated and then turned our skis so we could zag in the other direction. That next step was to begin hiring and adding additional resources, as I'll discuss in the next chapter.

SUMMARY

When you are driving to profitability in zig number 1, follow the basic components. Set a financial target and figure out

FIVE

Zag Number 2—Adding Processes and Resources

I love the Taj Mahal. I've had the good fortune to visit this remarkable shrine several times, and neither words nor pictures can describe it. What adds to its magnificence is that I've always come straight from the chaos of India, where there is mayhem everywhere, and to walk into this peaceful grove is like walking into another world.

The Taj Mahal was built with a labor force of over twenty thousand workers who were recruited from all across northern India and other parts of the region. In addition to common laborers, the workforce included sculptors from Bukhara, calligraphers from Syria and Persia, inlayers from southern India, and stonecutters from Baluchistan. A team of 37 men formed the creative unit. Of these, one was a specialist in carving marble flowers and another was the best at building turrets. It took 20 years to complete the Taj Mahal. It was built by Mughal Emperor Shah Jahan in memory of his beloved third wife Mumtz Mahal. It is considered one of the most beautiful buildings in the world and is a symbol of eternal love.

Imagine for a moment the possibility of this emperor trying to build the Taj Mahal all by himself. He clearly had a vision of what it was to be. He was a very wealthy man, so he had the necessary cash. And likely he knew where to find the materials from which this edifice was constructed. Despite all that he had at his disposal, building the Taj Mahal would have been an impossible feat, even if Shah Jahan had had several lifetimes in which to complete the work.

Instead, he put together his beacon in the fog, fueled it with his passion, and then added resources—lots and lots of resources. And as he added those resources, he had to get everyone to catch the same vision so they could complete something that beautiful.

ADDING RESOURCES

In the first zig, you made your business or your life profitable. Zag number 2 is about adding resources. Once you have enough cash from the first zig, you can use it to add those people, equipment, and other resources that you need. You need to do so in order to help perform the labor-intensive work that keeps the cash flowing. Then you are able to spend more of your time defining the processes and adding meat to the bones of your organization. This is the time to formalize, structure, and expand those things that led you to your initial success in zig number 1.

Getting to cash feels great! Your determination has begun to bear fruit. You're in the black. Life is good. You're actually making money. The only problem is you're completely worn out. And your gas tank is now on fumes, if not completely empty. You know you need to make a change, but you're also sensing how hard it is going to be to let go of some of your control and bring others on board. Doing so requires that you shift gears dramatically, and if you don't you'll never get to your destination.

Adding resources is harder than it sounds, but it's the only way you'll build your dream. I have a neighbor who owns a shoe repair shop. This man makes a decent living and takes care of his family's basic needs. However, to keep his head above water, he has to work day after day, week after week, repairing those shoes single-handedly. If he needs a day off, he has to close the shop. Same if he's under the weather or has to take care of a sick wife or child. Of course, that leads to a loss of income. Now, his business model allows for some days off, but it's a pretty thin margin. If something major happened, the effects could be catastrophic.

My friend has made it through zig number 1 profitability—but he has not thought to turn his skis in the other direction for zag number 2. In other words, he has not added the resources that would allow him to live a fuller, richer, and safer life.

A key reason many people have a hard time adding resources is they have become accustomed to micromanaging every aspect of their business. As hard as it can be to let go of control, as you hire the right people to fill in the gaps of knowledge or skill that you don't have, and then as you help them learn your processes, your company will begin to reach its full potential. Think of yourself as being akin to Emperor Shah Jahan, who may not have known how to carve flowers out of stone but was able to hire someone to do that job—and thus help him create his masterpiece.

I'm familiar with a family-owned business, run by a father and his sons, where the father has micromanaged every aspect of the business. The father is now getting old and is about to retire. He has talented sons who want to modernize the business, but his response is always, "We have been doing business this way for over forty years. This is how it has to be done." When the sons bring up the need to modernize equipment or processes, the father adamantly refuses.

It's no wonder the sons and their families are frustrated. They feel stuck in a business that is archaic, and they would like a little leeway in bringing the business into the computer age and making it more productive.

This example is common among family-run businesses, but the same plight is apparent among businesses founded by a strong-minded personality, who is then unwilling to bring in additional resources and let them do what they were hired to do. As you begin to take zag number 2 in order to grow your business, remembering that it is all about discipline will help you loosen your grip on the controls. The image I keep in mind to help me do this (because, I'll admit it, I can be a bit controlling) is what I call the "Yes, Yes, Yes, NO! Principle." While you are working on zig number 1 and trying to get to cash, you will, of necessity, say "Yes" to many things, such as:

⇨ Yes, I will do the accounting.

⇨ Yes, I will sell a small order that has potential for larger orders.

⇨ Yes, I will answer the phones.

⇨ Yes, I will take out the trash.

⇨ No, I will not compromise my values.

Now, as you add resources, it's time to add a few more "Nos." Some of these might be:

⇨ No, I will not take out the trash. I will hire a cleaning person.

⇨ No, I will not do my own accounting. I will outsource my taxes to an accountant.

⇨ No, I will not answer the phones and do the bookkeeping. I will hire an administrative assistant.

HIRING SMART

As you add resources to your business or your life, you still need to keep your cash flow heading in the right direction. Obviously, you don't want to begin hiring if doing so is going to put you in the red. But as you hire, you need to be clear in your mind, and with those you hire, that if the business becomes less profitable, you will have to decrease resources. This may seem harsh, but if you have employees in your organization who are not getting you to cash, it puts the whole company at risk. It is better to lay off those people who are not performing or creating value so you can create opportunities for more employees in the long run.

I was a middle manager in a company that hired a lot of employees but did not become profitable. That company waited until it was completely out of money and had declared bankruptcy before telling the employees they were out of jobs. To add insult, the employees were let go without being paid for their last month of work. Blind bliss is not bliss at all. It would have been much better for every person in that company to have been laid off when the problems started so they could begin their new job search, rather than wasting a month doing work for which they would never be paid.

In your life, you have to do the same thing. When you get to cash, you can spend a little more money adding resources such as a house, a car, a computer, or just some things that will make your life nicer and more efficient. When times get tight, you need to immediately tighten your budget and stop adding those resources. If times get really tight, you might have to sell off that nice car to make ends meet. The key is to always keep a close eye on your bottom line. Always stay profitable. If you're creative as you think about adding resources, you may be able to make more progress and spend less money.

When we began to add resources to CastleWave, the business Ron and I bootstrapped with only $5,000, our first significant hires were not college graduates. They were not even college students; they were nerdy sixteen- and seventeen-year-old high school boys. In our drive to profitability, I needed to add the resource of engineers. I knew I couldn't afford to hire engineers at the going rate, and I also knew I could train people who had a working knowledge of computers and the Internet to do what needed to be done. It hit me one day that my labor force could be found among my teenaged sons' friends. My only concern was that I needed them to have a strong vision, so I told them, "When you walk in this door each day, you're no longer seventeen. You're an MBA graduate from Harvard, and I expect you to behave like one." And guess what? They did exactly that. They grasped what I needed them to do, and they bought into the company culture. It probably didn't hurt that we paid them far more than they could have earned flipping burgers, but for a number of strategic reasons, those kids were so excited to come to work, they would sleep on the couch some nights because they were totally vested in what we were trying to do.

On the flipside, at this same time I made a couple of horrific hires, in part because we didn't have our value system clearly in place. During this time I was literally living off three to four hours of sleep a night. I hired an executive assistant who had a good resume, but what impressed me even more were her outstanding grades and recommendations. I had some concern that her work experience was a bit thin; but I needed someone quickly, so I hired her assuming her grades indicated a solid work ethic.

One week while my partner, Ron, and I were working a trade show in Florida, I kept trying to call into my office. I tried at several different times, but I just could not make contact with my new assistant. I finally called another recent hire who was supposed to be at the office. She did call me right back and said she was on a short lunch break and would call me back, which she failed to do. After four days of not being able to reach anyone, I called my wife and asked if she would go by the office and find out what was going on. When she arrived, the front door was locked and all of the lights were off. She found the main telephone was set to voice message. She did find an engineer in a back room, where he was working on a project. When she asked him what was going on, he told her that these two women, who were supposed to be answering my phones and greeting people, had decided that since I was gone that they would "work from home" that week.

Needless to say, I had to terminate both these women when I returned from my business trip. I made the mistake of hiring two young women who weren't hungry for the work I offered and who had a safety net at home that would rescue them. I also made the mistake of not screening them effectively against my organizational values, one of which is that we value hard workers.

Since that experience, I have learned to not be too busy to pay close attention as I add resources. I've also developed a series of questions and skills assessments that I run potential hires through, especially my executive admin, who I believe is my most important hire.

One of my best hires is a woman named Colette Marx. She is a mother who, by mutual agreement, is working for me from her home (which is yet another way to conserve resources). When I hired her, I gave her a copy of my book, *Bootstrap Business*, and told her she needed to read it and then take a test. The other people I hired at the same time all went home and skimmed through the book. But Colette wanted to succeed at this job; so she read the book, and then she went back and read the book again, this time highlighting it and making copious notes. When she brought it into the office to take the test, it was dog-eared, it was tagged, it was well used. Not surprisingly, Colette scored a perfect score. She's the only one to have done that. (She even scored higher than I did, and I wrote the book!) Colette didn't come with the strongest resume or the most extensive experience, but she is one of the most committed and engaged employees I have ever had.

OTHER RESOURCES TO ADD

Your organization will need resources other than more people. Resources can include more capital or a new piece of equipment that will simplify your processes. For example, if I were to create a cookie company, once I made enough money selling my first batch of cookies, I would consider using that money to purchase a machine that mixes the dough and then another one that cuts the cookies—after looking carefully at their cost and the potential return on my investment.

Outsourcing is another way to add resources. I started a company a year ago with my son. My son created a website, and we then outsourced the task of building five or six more websites. We gave the developer our website template and told her exactly how we wanted our sites to be built. Then we focused on other more lucrative parts of the venture. One good thing about outsourcing is that you don't have to worry as much about the value system. The high production or the end result is what matters when you outsource. The key to outsourcing is that you only want to outsource those things that can be thrown over the wall to someone who can do them independently. Do not try to outsource those things that require your full involvement. For example, I would not want to outsource my company's financial books. There are so many moving parts in my books that my executive admin and I must go through them daily. I want to know when bills go out, when we will be paid, and when our bills are due.

One time I tried to outsource one of my companies' bookkeeping to someone I knew in town. It ended up being a nightmare because I was no longer able to know at a moment's notice exactly where I stood financially. On the other hand, I do outsource my payroll. We send the payroll agency the hours each of my employees work, and they take care of all the required forms and paperwork. I also outsource my taxes to my accountant. We just send him a copy of our QuickBooks and the year-end papers, and he can take care of our taxes without taking any of my time.

BUILDING PROCESSES

Now that you've started bringing in some cash and adding resources, your organization is going to need more structure and discipline. As you add more flesh to the bones of your infrastructure, you'll need to work on making consistent progression. This will require that you build on what you have learned so far as you have been driving to profitability. In some cases, those will be lessons you haven't even realized you've learned.

Building processes for your organization is vital to your short-term and long-term viability. It's a step that often gets left out as you head toward your beacon in the fog, but I've been convinced of its importance since I was a little kid mowing lawns. After I had acquired a few lawn mowers and convinced my brothers and friends to mow lawns for me, I had to teach them the processes that had made me successful in the first place. Here are the steps I took each and every time I mowed a customer's lawn:

1. Present yourself well. I would tuck in my shirt and wipe the sweat and dirt off my hands and face before knocking on the customer's door with a big smile on my face and saying, "Hello, I am here to mow your lawn today. It will take me about an hour and a half. Is now an okay time?"

2. Clear the lawn. Before mowing a lawn, I looked it over carefully and removed all the balls and junk. I picked up any dog mess, trash, or anything else that may be on the lawn.

3. Trim the lawn. I used the trimmer to trim around the entire edge of the lawn before I began mowing.

4. Check the oil in the lawn mower.

5. Check the gas in the lawn mower and make sure the tank is full. I only put gas in the lawn mower while it was on the sidewalk so that I didn't kill any grass if I spilled.

6. I went to the center of the lawn and picked a point straight across the lawn. Then I shot for a straight line. Everyone likes nice straight lines better than random tire marks across their lawns.

7. I followed the wheel patterns through the entire lawn to keep all of the lines straight. If the lines got off, I corrected them.

8. I emptied the grass bag before it got full so that clumps of grass would not spill out on the lawn.

9. After mowing, I cleaned up the lawn and yard. I raked any grass or debris that was left on the lawn and blew or swept the sidewalks off. Everyone likes their yard to look neat and clean after the grass is mowed.

10. I respectfully invoiced the customer. I wiped the sweat off my face and the dirt off my hands and knocked on the customer's door. I then handed them the invoice for mowing the lawn and put a piece of candy or a package of seeds with it as I thanked them for the opportunity of mowing their lawn.

This process example may seem rather elementary, but I had to mow a lot of lawns before I learned that it took a lot less time and the lawn looked much neater if I trimmed the edges before I mowed. I also learned that when I was having other people mow lawns for me, they all wanted to do it their own way. But I knew that my customers had hired me to mow their lawns because they knew they would have straight lines and they would like the way their lawn looked after it was mowed. They also loved that I gave them a packet of seeds or a piece of candy as my signature when I finished. So, I had to document the processes and teach these things to my employees so they would know what my customers expected.

My wife worked for Kentucky Fried Chicken while she was a teenager. They have a list posted to the wall above the biscuit machine detailing the exact steps for making their delicious, fluffy biscuits as well as other lists detailing each step in making their chicken and every other menu item. This keeps the consistency and quality that is expected each time a customer goes to eat at any KFC.

I used to love to eat at a regional fast-food restaurant that sells delicious chicken and rice bowls. But one time when I went there, the dish I was served did not taste the same. I commented to the person at the counter, "Something tastes really weird in my chicken." He said, "Oh, yeah, our normal supplier was out of the chicken we normally use, so we had to use different chicken today." I thought this was just a fluke, so I went back the following week. This time the chicken tasted much spicier than usual, and it was even worse than the previous week. I mentioned it to the guy at the front again and he said, "Yes, we had to try an even different supplier this week." I went back a few more times, but each time the chicken was different. Not surprisingly, this franchise went out of business not long after, and now I have to drive 30 miles to get the chicken and rice that I love. Whatever the size or complexity of your business, processes matter!

In zag number 2, you have to document the processes that led to your initial success. You need to put these into bite-sized processes that other people can follow. That is why I instructed my employees to trim the grass before they mowed the lawn and put the gas into the mower while it was on cement so as to not kill the grass. I had made all these mistakes and had learned from them, so I institutionalized what I had learned.

As you document your processes, remember to learn from the mistakes you made driving to profitability. Documenting what *not* to do is as important as documenting what to do. You want to have something in place that makes people think twice about making the same mistakes, and it will help if you have already proven what doesn't work.

The Five-Minute Whiteboard

One of the powerful tools I use in my business is the Five-Minute Whiteboard. This is designed to ensure that everyone on the team knows which of our tasks are the 20 percent that will result in 80 percent of the results. It works for a team of up to seven or eight members.

I've installed a huge whiteboard in our office. We write each team member's name across the top with a different color of marker. In our staff meetings, each person then brain dumps everything they have to do during the coming week. It doesn't matter whether it is a small little thing or a really big thing—we list everything. After everyone has listed their tasks, they then put an "A" "B" or "C" next to each task to give it a priority ("A" for vital, "C" not so much).

We then all stand back and look over the board. We're then able to see that if this person doesn't get something done, this other person won't be able to get her highest priority done. We also discuss if items need a higher priority or if they are not really that important.

As the week goes on, each team member crosses off completed tasks. They also have the ability to write on someone else's list. If there is a task anywhere on the board that is critical to you, you can increase its priority. I have even put big red circles around someone's task, letting them know that it is getting to be a hot potato in the business and that they need to deal with it. When one team member's list is getting shorter, they're expected to help someone else with their list and cross off items.

There are three very powerful functions that this Five-Minute Whiteboard fills:

1.   Instantly, everyone on the team knows what the critical tasks are for the week.

2.   The team knows when someone is overburdened, and they can help him or her out. If John has 15 "A" items on his list, the rest of the team knows not to dump more onto him. If Matt only has a few smaller items, he knows he must help John.

3.   It provides accountability and transparency in the organization, which ensures that everyone is actually producing and being effective.

I have found that the Five-Minute Whiteboard is the most powerful when we do it on a Friday afternoon rather than the first thing Monday morning. This allows everyone to subconsciously begin thinking through their task lists so that on Monday morning they are geared up and ready to attack.

Recently, I witnessed yet one more example of how effective our Five-Minute Whiteboard is. We had a situa-

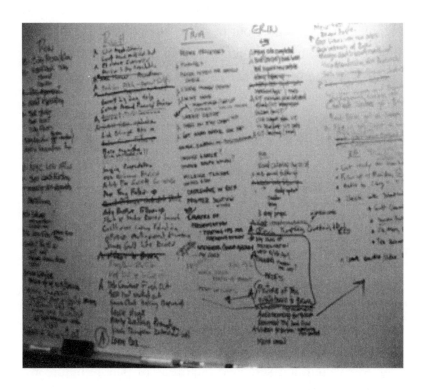

tion where we had a large shipment that had been stalled due to some shipping infrastructure issues. As a result, we had $150,000 worth of merchandise just sitting in our warehouse waiting to be shipped—and holding up our cash flow. The day finally came when the truck was able to come, but it showed up two-and-a-half hours earlier than scheduled. Loading this truck and getting this shipment off was an "A+" item on our warehouse manager's list. When the truck showed up early, not one word was said. Everyone on the team just got up, put on their coats and gloves, and went out into the cold parking lot to help Cameron load the truck. Everyone knew this shipment was critical to our business and essential to the cash flow. Everyone understood and was in tune with the environment of the company. That is the power of the Five-Minute Whiteboard.

EATING OUR OWN COOKING

In our test business, we hit profitability one month ahead of schedule. We then documented processes, which helped ensure that when we began hiring people, they would actually know what to do. Shane, our college student who was so helpful in the beginning, graduated from college and was able to join us full-time. The next person we hired was Koral, my executive admin. I believe this hire is always the most important. We vetted and screened hundreds of people before we found Koral. She has been a perfect fit with our values, and she has brilliant skills. She is now the gatekeeper of our values and does a screening of every person who enters our organization. She makes sure that they are a value fit.

To help document the process that made our company profitable, I identified 12 parts of our operations that needed to be managed in order for us to be successful. I took pieces of paper and wrote one of these items on each piece of paper, and then stapled each to a $20 bill and posted these around the office. I told everyone that the first person who wrote up the process for that step got to keep the $20 bill. We now have 12 documented processes, each with its own set of simple steps written out so that each new person who joins the business has a clear picture of what needs to be done to make our company work.

After hiring Koral and a few other key positions, my partner Curtis needed to hire a very important individual for our sales team. At this point, we had created our values filter, and we had the skills test assembled to give to our future hires. Curtis was thoughtful and pragmatic as he ran a large number of candidates through this process, even though we had an urgent need to fill this position. After screening all the candidates, one in particular stood out. He was very talented and had the skills we needed. He had passed all of our tests. I told Curtis to just hire the guy, but Curtis slowed down just a little because he saw some red flags.

Some of the red flags had to do with this individual's work history. He had not had real consistency in his employment. We figured we could overlook this because we knew he had dealt with some health problems. Another red flag was that in our interviews, this man seemed to have more motion than momentum. Even so, I was convinced this guy was a good hire, but Curtis was still concerned. After I kept prodding him, Curtis decided to extend the offer. As Curtis and the man were talking on the phone, Curtis could hear the man's wife in the background. She was shouting things like "If you agree to accept this, make sure they let you work from home two days a week!" We hadn't discussed that in the interviews, but Curtis thought it might work. Then Curtis heard her say, "Make sure the health insurance kicks in immediately!" That was fine because we offer a good health insurance package.

Then he heard her say, "Find out how many vacation days they're giving you, and then ask for a week more." In a bad economy with a lot of competition for this position, there was no gratitude or excitement about the offer. There was no dialogue about how he was going to add value to our company. It was all about take, take, take. After four or five of these demands, Curtis paused and simply said, "I'm sorry, we're not moving forward." He knew our company's values, and he knew we would not be adding a resource that fit. Even though we really needed this position filled, Curtis went back to the drawing board and started all over. Fortunately, we soon found a delightful woman named Chiaki who fit our needs perfectly. She is aligned with our company values and has been the right hire for this job.

SUMMARY

After you have hit profitability in zig number 1, zag number 2 is all about adding resources. You are making the transition from working harder to working smarter. You are going from determination to discipline. You are going from being the butcher, the baker, and the candlestick maker to cheerleading a team and turning over control to others. Remember that this will involve letting your hires make some mistakes and do things a little differently than you would. But if you do this effectively, you are increasing your profitability, adding resources into the system, and documenting the processes.

This is where the culture of your company will be defined. It's one of the most fun phases of your business, where stories will come that will define the life of your business—good and bad! Your values will be tested for the first time, so hold strong.

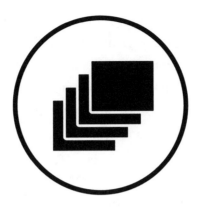

SIX

Zig Number 3— Adding Scale

The third zig is about adding scale to your undertaking. After getting to cash and then adding resources and processes, you need to add scale to get your product or services to the masses. In simple terms, scale is something that can be published or duplicated or sold over and over again. Think about the music industry as an example. There are amazingly talented studio musicians who get hired to play for top recording artists. They come into the studio, lay down their tracks, get a check for an awful lot of money, and then go on to their next gig. They live a good life, making more than most of us. The trouble is their check is a one-time payment. On the other hand, the artist who writes and records the song gets a royalty every time the song is downloaded, sold at Wal-Mart, or played on the radio. Through scaling their talents and business strategies, recording artists get *lots and lots* of checks for an awful lot of money—and live a *great* life!

Business gets really fun for me when I can make money while I'm sleeping, or on vacation, or working on my next project. I remember the first time this happened for me. I was laid up in bed for what I knew was going to be a few weeks, so I came up with a little business idea, threw together a website, worked my search engine optimization magic, and went to bed. I got up the next morning, brushed my teeth, checked the website, and found I had made $37.50—while I had been asleep! (That number got bigger as the days went on.) Scale is what allows me to do that.

My colleagues and I often use the phrase "Nail it, then scale it." What we mean is that during the first two zigs and zags, you're really trying to figure out how to nail your business. You're figuring out the discipline, the effort, and the processes that will make it work. In zig number 1, you are figuring out how to get to profitability. In zag number 2, you are adding resources. In zig number 3, you need to figure out a model that you can replicate quickly and get your product out to the masses. This is the "scaling it" part.

When I've talked or written about this concept, I've offended several members of my family because I summarize my ideas by stating, "I never want to be a doctor and certainly never a lawyer!" My point is not to offend my brother, who is a very successful doctor. My point is that doctors have to put on their literal rubber gloves and poke at some very tender places, and attorneys have to put on their figurative rubber gloves and poke in some dark places. Otherwise, neither one is making money. I don't want to do that. I like making money beyond the time that I am physically and/or mentally working.

There are alternatives most of us can pursue, though. I have a good friend who is a dentist. He's told me several times about a really great product he wants to develop that would make it so much easier to fill cavities. He has lamented that he just doesn't have enough time to work on this because he is stuck drilling and filling teeth all day long. He feels he has no options, but I've explained that the option is to zigzag. He already has a business with a solid cash flow. He just needs to add resources—and then scale.

One way would be to bring another dentist into his practice so he could take Fridays off to work on creating his new product. He could then join forces with other local practices to build a channel or infrastructure to test and promote his new product. When that has proven successful, he could create an online presence. When we talked about his options, my friend was amazed that he could take control of his own destiny and move from the constrained "I'm going to spend the rest of my life drilling teeth" mind-set to the "I can actually pursue my beacon in the fog" mind-set.

While others see limitations, I see examples of scale all around me. I found one while attending a retreat being run by a well-known chiropractor. This man is clearly an exceptionally talented chiropractor who had become very profitable in his practice. He then added resources and staff and was able to add several additional offices to his practice. Then he made the big leap to scale. He compiled his own set of processes that worked in his business, including the equipment he used, the supplements he recommended, and the processes that made him successful. He put all of this together into a system he could sell to other chiropractors. This man is now distinctly known for his training programs among chiropractors throughout the United States. With his training program, he helps other chiropractors—and then profits when they tell their associates about what he's done for them. But he has no direct involvement in their day-to-day businesses. This is scale.

My oldest son seems to have gotten some of my genes, which led to him getting involved in my web businesses several years ago. (He was one of my original nerdy kids who helped me move CastleWave forward.) After I sold CastleWave, he wanted to start his own business. He worked hard to follow the principles and processes he learned at CastleWave and ended up building a scalable web business of his own. He is now in Japan for two years working as an unpaid service volunteer, and he has a business that is still making money for him. While he is gone, his 17-year-old brother is the CEO of the company. He also hired his younger brother and several other smart and energized teenagers to keep his business going— and growing. They have the same values in place. They have their beacon in the fog set and are fueled with the passion of youth. As I write this, my son has been gone for 13 months, and he has a resource and an asset that will fund the remainder of his college when he returns. That is the power of scale.

THE FOUR RULES OF SCALE

I have developed four rules I follow whenever I create a business. There are times I violate them, but I do so deliberately. Keep in mind that these are *my* rules that fit into *my* skill set and values. You will need to look at your own situation and determine the rules that work for you.

RULE # 1—RIDE A WAVE

I like businesses that are on a wave. Just like a surfer who gets in front of a wave and rides it to the shore, I want the environment to be right before I get on a wave in my business or my life. If the wave is big enough, then just being in its vicinity will generate enough power to propel you toward your destination. But if you catch that wave wrong, life can come crashing down around you. The key is to get on and off the wave at the right time. September 12, 2001, would have been a terrible time to start an airline. This same day would have been the perfect time to start an antiterrorist airline security business. Purchasing a row of new condos in 2006, when housing prices were at a point where experts were beginning to see they were unsustainable, would have been a bad move. Purchasing those same condos after the housing bubble burst and prices were slashed in half would have been the right time to add scale. You need to assess your environment and pick the right waves to ride.

RULE #2—TRANSACTION BUSINESSES

I like businesses that sit in the middle of a transaction. A well-known example is credit card companies, which make 2 to 5 percent every time one of us slides our credit card through a reader. None of us give what we're paying a thought (and if you think we're not paying, think again). Merchants are happy to pass along the fee because the convenience brings more people to their business. Customers love the convenience of not having to carry cash or write a check, so they willingly pay their annual fee (and high interest rates, as well). Positioning yourself in the middle of a transaction puts you in a great place to make money.

RULE #3—OWN THE CUSTOMER

I like to own the customer. I don't like being in a business where I can't look into the eyeballs of the customer and resolve the issue. I like to be in the middle of the transaction, but I do not like being sandwiched between brokers.

During the rise in the housing market, I was riding a great wave with a company called Mortgage Saver 101. We had an awesome website that generated leads of people looking to obtain mortgages. The company was riding a wave and was a transactional and a digital business. The only problem was that we did not sell our leads directly to the banks or the people who were coming to refinance their loans. We sold our leads to a broker who would then sell them to multiple vendors. Many times the broker would come back to us and say he did not like some of our leads. We would ask what he didn't like, and he would simply say, "It wasn't a quality lead." Without being able to talk to the bank or the customer, we were left to guess at what they really wanted. This left us very vulnerable, giving all of the power to the broker. If there was a problem, we had no way to solve it. On the other hand, credit card companies are good examples of being able to own the customer. The credit card company can communicate directly with the merchant that is selling the product or the customer that has signed up for the credit card. They own the customer. They can manage the relationship on both sides of the transaction.

Rule #4—I Like Digital Assets

This is my very personal preference, but I love digital assets. I really do not like retail. Why? Because I stink at retail. I don't have enough discipline, and I am not patient enough to succeed in retail. It doesn't scale as well for me. I know many other people who have been highly successful in retail, but it is just not my preference. Once I build a website or a digital application, I only have to make it one time. Then an unlimited number of people can go to my webstie or click on my toolbar. In a retail store, there is a limit to how many people can fit into the store and how many people are able to find the store. With digital assets there are so many more options. That's the primary reason I like digital assets.

I do have some businesses that do not fit according to these last two rules, but have been very stable businesses that have scaled well. My wife and I started purchasing rental properties many years ago. We bought our first fourplex at a fire sale after the owners went bankrupt. We put enough money down that the cash started flowing from the moment we bought it. As we obtained more cash, we paid off this property. Through trial and error, we have been through the learning curve to know how to manage these rentals. With the money we made from that first rental, we bought another rental property. We added resources by hiring a repairman and other people to help manage the properties. We hired our sons to work on these rentals, as this was a great way to teach them how to work hard. (I'd hire my daughters, but we don't have any.) One by one, we purchased rental properties that got us to cash, paid them off, and then purchased more. The great thing about these properties is that they are income-producing assets. Even as the housing market took a nosedive, our rentals remained full. Those people who no longer qualified for mortgages needed places to live and were happy to live in our rentals.

When my partners and I started CastleWave, we first got our initial SEO contracts to drive us to profitability, and then we hired the engineers we needed to build our resources. Then it was time to add scale. The scale component in CastleWave was our link-building component—the ability to get other authoritative websites to direct traffic to the sites for which we were consulting. Our expertise in this area was our number one value asset. We put together a pragmatic system—a set of processes and approaches that were bundles—that we could then have our employees replicate and follow, allowing my partners and me to focus on other issues.

If done properly, scale allows you to develop a system and train other people in how to use that system. Put together an entire system and process using all your rules of engagement, and then flip the switch and start cranking out the cookies. A cookie-cutter system is what will get you to scale.

Microsoft Windows is a great example of scale. How many times did Microsoft build Windows? Yes, Bill Gates and company have released updates and improvements (well, most of the time), but they really only built the program once! And they have been able to sell it millions and millions of times over. Virtually every PC sold has Microsoft Windows already installed, and Microsoft gets a royalty each time a person opens their box. Now that is scale—and the reason why Bill Gates is one of the richest men in the world!

BREAKING DOWN OF THE CONCEPT

Zig number 3 requires yet another shift in mind-set. In zig number 1 you are doing everything, and you are working hard. In zag number 2, you become the head cheerleader, and you are defining processes. Zig number 3 requires deliberate planning. It is very cerebral. It is the academic part. It's a shift that is hard for many people to go through. Working hard and working cerebral don't always go well together unless you consciously acknowledge these two forces and plan the expenditure of your energy accordingly.

As you shift to your cerebral effort, you are standing back from the minutia, analyzing it, and determining what little levers you could flip that would have significant impact. In other words, you're deliberately thinking, "If I do such and such to the business, then we can accomplish this." Up until now, your efforts have been all about action. Now you're looking for ways to maximize the work being done and for ways to shift your work to others.

One of my recent ventures involved building an e-mail list of several thousand subscribers. That's not a huge number, but for this particular niche we had amassed a sizeable database. We had gone about building this list in a hundred or more different ways. We tried one thing, and if it failed, we tried another. We worked fast and we worked hard, which meant we didn't always refine our efforts to the point of perfection. In fact, in many cases we settled for "good enough." This is what my friend meant when he said he was "striving for mediocrity."

After we had built our e-mail database to what we determined was our critical mass, we set about to craft the pitch that had always been our endgame. We had one chance—an e-mail blast that, if people responded, would bring us the success we had been building toward.

At this point, our strategy shifted from action to considerable thought. "Good enough" no longer was. Whereas early on we had thrown together things that took literally minutes, we now spent hours and hours on this one pitch, running our final effort through layers of strategic review and approval.

I can't tell you exactly where you'll need to expend your cerebral capital. What I can do is encourage you to carve out time to step back, get away, and do the thinking that will identify where you can focus, refine, add resources, create processes, and move toward the scale that will create value whether you're in the office or enjoying the fruits of your efforts.

I can also tell you this. I have had very little success getting to a scale component when I'm in a crisis or in a reactionary mode. I'm great at solving problems, but I am lousy at coming up with new ideas when I am in that task-oriented, problem-solving mind-set. Find time to get away to a relaxed, calm atmosphere when you're generating ideas for how to scale your business. I have had enough ideas come while I am on the golf course to justify my green fees for the next 10 or 20 years.

THE DECISION MATRIX

When I am planning new ideas for my business or for my life, I like to use a tool I created called the Decision Matrix. It helps me decide which ideas or options fit into my value plan. This decision matrix can be used for any kind of decision you need to make in your life. I have used it to help me decide which jobs I should take, where I would like to live, and, yes, what businesses and scale ideas I should pursue. I love to use this model to appease the left hemisphere of my brain, which is the logical side. It does not always tell me exactly which option that I want to take, but it does help me weed out the options that are best not to take. It is really straightforward and simple.

Here's how it works. Across the top of the paper, spread-sheet or whiteboard, I compose a list of the top 10 or 15 (maximum) things that are important to me for the particular decision I am trying to make. For example, in a business some of the things I might want that business to do would include making me a lot of money, allowing me flexibility of lifestyle, giving back to society, or requiring international travel. If I were making a decision on where to buy a new home, I may list across the top things like location, quality of schools,

	BIG BACK YARD	SAFE NEIGHBORHOOD	HOME OFFICE	GOOD SCHOOLS	VIEWS	QUALITY	NICE KITCHEN	BASEMENT	NEAR SHOPPING	COMMUTE TO WORK	
WEIGHT PRIORITY FACTOR	1.6	1.9	1.4	2	1.3	1.5	1.7	1.2	1.1	1.8	
HOME#1	7	6	7	10	7	5	6	7	2	10	
HOME#2	4	8	9	5	2	10	9	3	2	6	
HOME#3	6	8	7	5	6	8	6	6	5	3	
HOME#4	5	8	8	8	10	2	9	6	7	4	
HOME #1	11.2	11.4	9.8	20	9.1	7.5	10.2	8.4	2.2	18	107.8
HOME #2	6.4	15.2	12.6	10	2.6	15	15.3	3.6	2.2	10.8	93.7
HOME #3	9.6	15.2	9.8	10	7.8	12	10.2	7.2	5.5	5.4	92.7
HOME #4	8	15.2	11.2	16	13	3	15.3	7.2	7.7	7.2	103.8

safety, friendliness of neighbors, quality of the construction, yard for the dog, a good view, and so on.

Once I have made my list across the top of the things that are most important to me in this decision, then I rate them in order of priority as to how important they are to me. The most important item would have a rating of 2. The next item would be ranked a 1.9, then 1.8, all the way down to the least important item.

In the business example, I may give "flexibility of lifestyle" a 1.8 rating and the "international travel," which I love but which may not be as important to me as my lifestyle, a 1.5 rating. If I were moving to a new house, I would rate the quality of schools a 2, where I might rate the view I desire a 1.2.

Once I have my values of what I desire listed across the top and weighted in order of priority, then I list down on the left side all of the options I am considering. If I am thinking of ideas that would scale my business, I would list all of those down the left side. If I were purchasing a house, I would list all of the different property options down that left side. If I were deciding which job opportunity I wanted to pursue or which college to attend, or whatever it is I am deciding, I would list the options down the left side.

After my chart is complete, I ignore the weight factor of those important items and I fill in the blanks. I just go through really quickly and assess to the best of my judgment how my idea or decision would rank with my important item. I use a score of 1 to 10, with 10 being the highest. After I have filled out the chart, I simply take the score of the idea to the important item and multiply it by the weighted factor of that idea. I then sum all of the important items together for a score of each idea.

If there are several people involved, then I have each person do their own weight factor. We add up the weight factors and then use that number to score the spreadsheet. Together we decide the score between 1 to 10 of how well that idea would fit our needs. If my wife wants a good view and I want a shorter commute to work, we would weigh those items differently.

I like to do this exercise when I am relaxed and calm. It takes about an hour or so, but it is a really precise and fun way to sort out my ideas. Oftentimes, I'll get the top four of five scoring ideas. These scores are not the only factors in my decisions, but they do usually tell me which of the options are not the ones that I want to pursue. It helps me to hone in a little bit to where I want to take my next zig or zag.

EATING OUR OWN COOKING

We are currently trying to figure out the scale phase in our Froghair business. When we initially defined our three zigs and zags, we defined our scale as making three sales into our direct channel each day. As we progressed, we hit profitability and were able to add resources, but we realized that our plan for scaling the business was not viable. So, we had to adjust our strategy and go after a second option. This time our plan was to sell items to large companies to use as their corporate gifts. This has had some success, but we are still exploring other options. Specifically, we are looking at generating Internet leads in our area of the market. Almost every day we're using the zig zag principle because it gives us the flexibility to adjust and change course within the boundaries that we have set. As we've seen obstacles, we've skied around them. And we've been prepared to do so because we know they're going to come. My experience has taught me there is a much higher probability of success when you use this principle.

SUMMARY

Zig number 3 involves a major shift in mind-set. You are no longer working *in* your business; you are working *on* your

business. You are becoming deliberate, and you have struc-
tures in place. You've survived the determination phase.
You've survived the discipline phase. Now you can leverage
yourself, leverage the value of the market you're in, and start
to really see some success.

Boundaries and Guardrails

As you zigzag down that mountain toward your goal, you
need to realize there are hazards on either side of the
ski run. Ski resorts groom and prepare the areas intended for
skiers; however, experienced skiers know that just beyond the

groomed runs are trees, rocks, potential avalanches, cliffs, and other dangers that may cause injury or even death. The same is true in business and life. If we're smart, we establish boundaries and guardrails to keep us away from perils and on the groomed slopes that lead to our goals.

Some people think zigzagging is easy or a lazy person's game. The reality is it requires great discipline and control. Any skier will tell you that traversing a steep mountain requires a strong back and legs, quick reflexes, and agility, while heading straight down is far less taxing. That is, until you crash and burn.

To avoid disaster, you're going to want to create boundaries and set guardrails, which will keep you headed in the direction of your goal—and away from your own personal train wreck.

KEEPING YOUR ZIGZAGS UNDER CONTROL

When you are beginning to head toward your beacon in the fog, you want to concentrate on three zigs and zags at a time. That will keep you focused and under control. To help you with that, think in terms of devoting 65 percent of your time and resources on zig number 1 (driving to profitability), with 25 percent spent on planning and preparing for zag number 2 (adding resources and processes once you get to cash). The final 10 percent of your time and resources should be spent planning how you want to scale your undertaking in zig number 3 (creating scale). If you're looking beyond three zigs, life gets too complex.

Once you have hit zig number 1 and your business is profitable, you need to turn and head toward zag number 2. It's easy, once you have cash coming in, to think you can skip making the turn. But if you just stay in zig number 1, you may miss out on the dreams and goals defined as your true beacon in the fog. (And remember, cash alone is not a beacon worth pursuing.)

Once you are profitable, you should shift and spend about 65 percent of your time and energy on zag number 2, with 25 percent of your time spent on planning and preparing for zig number 3. Again, if you do not make this next turn, you may find yourself with a lot of resources, but never hitting that big goal. The last 10 percent of your time and efforts can then go toward setting another series of zigs that will help you get even closer to your beacon in the fog.

Remember, as you're zigzagging, to look for dangers or pitfalls that are in your way. There have been lots of times when I've been skiing on a run I thought I knew well, only to spot a rock or bare spot that has reared its ugly head. By remaining agile and in control, you can avoid whatever obstacle is lurking.

In the current business Curtis and I are working on, we began by setting our goal and then laying out our zigs and zags. Our first two zigs were clear, but our third zag was way off in the distance. As we hit profitability and then began working on adding resources, it became evident that our initial plan did not have as high a probability of success as several other opportunities we had uncovered as we were working through our first two zigs. So, we adjusted, which you should always keep as an option.

What you do not want to change, however, is the present target you are shooting for. Keeping control of your zigs will help you stay focused on that target, rather than turning hither and yon whenever the urge presents itself. In my experience, if you begin thinking beyond three zigs, you will actually lose sight of the path you are on. It will probably take you more than three zigs and zags to get to your final beacon in the fog, but only look out at three at one time. As you complete each goal, take a minute to celebrate, but then climb a tree and look out above the fog toward your beacon, making certain you are still on course. Then set another zig that will lead you in the direction you need to go.

A common question I hear is, "If I am making money, why do I want to make the next turn? Wouldn't it be better to just keep making money?" I have seen many examples of people who just kept chasing cash. Often, these are small, family-owned businesses where mom and dad are working day and night. They make enough money to cover their expenses or maybe to live comfortably; but by not adding resources, they never seem to be able to enjoy life away from the shop.

I have a neighbor who owns a candy-making business. He is the only one who knows how to make the candy. His wife works in the front, taking orders and keeping the books. This is a very labor-intensive business that requires this couple to work every day. They've lamented to me on many occasions that they never dare take a day off to go on a vacation or to enjoy their life because they are afraid of what their absence will do to the business. Just think what they could do if they would go to the next zig, document their processes, hire a few employees, and grow their company, even just a little. When people won't make the turn after hitting zig number 1, they get stuck—even though they may have a bunch of cash.

Everyone's situation is different in significant ways; but, as you create your own set of guardrails to control your zigs and zags, here are some common elements to include.

1. **A financial number**. How much money are you willing to spend on each zig? If you do not hit your goal within this budget, you are not profitable and may have to check your idea off as a failure. Do not chase losing bets.

2. **An allocation of time**. How much of your time are you willing to dedicate toward each individual zig? I like to spend 65 percent of my working time on the current zig. I then spend 25 percent and 10 percent planning out the next zigs and zags, respectively, that I will take. If I'm spending more than that, I reassess.

3. **Duration of time**. How long are you willing to work on this venture before hitting your financial target? Are you going to chase cash for a month, a year, or 10 years?

4. **A financial target**. How much profit do you want to
    make before heading toward the next zig? How much
    will you need in order to pursue the next zag?

Building Your Guardrails

The guardrails you create must be closely aligned with the values you set in Chapter 3. You need to have people in your life who will tell you when you are out of bounds. I have a good friend who was a successful and well-known college basketball coach until he got embroiled in some politics and lost his job. We were talking, not long after that, and he shared what I consider to be a very profound insight. He said, "Rich, when I was winning championships, everyone laughed at my jokes. Now they only laugh when my jokes are actually funny." You need someone in your inner circle who knows you and whom you trust to tell you if your jokes are funny or not.

Alex Mendozian is a teleseminar trainer. We had discussed the possibility of working on a project together. Before we began, he called me and said, "Rich, I have some good news and some bad news. I'd really like to work with you. That is the good news. The bad news is, before I do, I need to have an intervention in your life." I pushed back, thinking, "What is he talking about? I don't have a drinking or a drug problem!" He continued, "Yes, you need an intervention!" He then got my wife and his executive assistant on the phone and explained he was having this intervention because I had to quit saying

"Yes" to everyone and everything. Warren Buffett once said, "The difference between successful people and very successful people is that very successful people say 'no' to almost everything" (Maddock, G. Michael & Viton, Raphael Louis, "The Stop-Doing List," *Bloomberg Businessweek*, December 7, 2010).

Sometimes, in your zeal to reach your beacon in the fog, everything seems possible. It's a time when you're generating a lot of ideas. It's a time when, out of necessity, you need to fire, fire, fire, and then aim. I refer to this part of zig number 1 as the time I have to weave gold out of straw. During this time, I may not have a lot of resources, and I may find myself holding things together with duct tape and bailing wire. As I'm trying to get something to work that will generate cash, I find myself saying, "Yes, yes, yes, no; . . . yes, yes, yes, maybe."

Once I get to the next zag, I have to create systematic and organized processes so I can hire employees and teach them how to make the business work. During this time, I find myself saying "No" about half the time. Part of that involves learning the discipline of delegating and letting others do the work for me.

Getting to the third zig demonstrates that I have achieved success by reaching cash, creating an organization that is working. Now I need to scale it. This is a much more controlled phase of the process because I do not want to destroy what I have just created. I finally have all of the gears meshing, and I now need to figure out how to scale the business so it will generate income independent of my direct involvement. During this period, I find myself needing to say "No" far more often.

Another guardrail you need to put in place is identifying and empowering those people in your life who will help you say "No" and who will let you know when you are heading out of bounds. For me, those people include my wife and my executive admin, both of whom are excellent at letting me know when I am crossing the lines I've established. My children will sometimes even tell me when I am out of line—and I've learned to listen. My business partner is another person I make sure I listen to. Unfortunately, it's rare that your subordinates will point out when you're heading toward danger. Some see things quite clearly, but many either are making sure they look good in your eyes or are afraid of your reaction. If one speaks up, listen, unless it feels like they're stroking your ego.

Staying Out of the Weeds

Weeds are diversions, inefficiencies, and even short-term successes that distract you from the course you have set for yourself. Weeds can be either negative or positive forces. They may take the form of being stuck with a large team that you just can't find a way to keep motivated. They might involve becoming so mesmerized with the profitability you've achieved that you forget to move on to your next step. Your personal weeds might have to do with a tendency to continually react to everyone else's demands instead of moving toward your goal.

Just as important as establishing the values that will serve as your road map is your need to set up the guardrails that will keep you out of the weeds. The guardrails you'll need to keep you out of the weeds are very personal and will differ according to your circumstances and objectives. Everyone should have guardrails in place for the various parts of each zig and zag so that you are always in control of your financial number, your allocation of time, your duration of time, and your financial target. Your other guardrails will be determined by factors such as your tolerance for risk, your family's tolerance for risk, your value system, and what portion of your personal network you are willing to expose to your endeavor.

I'm going to share some of my guardrails, but remember that these are *my* rules, not yours. I share them only to illustrate how important it is to give careful, specific thought to your guardrails, rather than attempting to put them in place when you're in the middle of heading over the cliff. Here are some of my guardrails:

- ⇨ I will not jeopardize the financial stability of my home or family. I am not going to mortgage my house for my business.

- ⇨ I like to keep my teams small (under 15 people).

- ⇨ I will be very careful in taking venture capital. I want to retain ownership in my companies.

- ⇨ I must control the finances of my business.

⇨ I will not sign personal guarantees on a business I do not personally control.

⇨ I will protect my personal network.

⇨ I will not get involved in a business that goes against my personal moral values.

⇨ I will not do anything illegal or unethical.

⇨ I will not work with people I do not enjoy. Whether it is a customer, a vendor, or an employee, life is too short to work with miserable people.

My list is actually longer, but these are a few examples of my guardrails. If I find myself getting near the edge on any of these, my wife, my business partner, and my executive admin each knows me well enough to tell me I am starting to cross the line. And I expect them not to stand by silently.

The following are brief elaborations on the rules I have set for myself—the reasons behind each guardrail. Again, remember that your circumstances and needs are different from mine, just as each ski slope is different. The key is that you need to define what guardrails you need in your life.

I WILL NOT RISK MY FAMILY'S FINANCIAL STABILITY

Before I took the plunge into full-time entrepreneurship, my wife and I had paid off our home. This was a huge milestone

for us, and it provided us with some sense of security as I
undertook pursuits that involved a much higher degree of risk.
I have committed that I will not jeopardize my home because
I do not want to take risks with my family's financial security.

I KEEP MY TEAMS SMALL

Whether I've been working for an organization or running
a small business, I have always preferred to keep my teams
small. I know myself well enough to know that this is where I
excel. I have found that if I keep my teams under 15 employees, then I can know the needs, interests, and desires of each
person. I can get to know what motivates them so I can push
the right buttons to keep each person going. I have run much
larger teams, but keeping them small results in the highest
output for the amount of input I can give.

I AVOID VENTURE CAPITAL TO
START OR GROW A BUSINESS

I have a good friend who had the courage to become an entrepreneur 15 years ago. He and his family came close to living
on wheat and water so he could create his business. He maxed
out credit cards and used whatever he had to become successful. And, indeed, he did become successful and profitable.
He and his business partner then decided to grow the com-

pany even bigger, and they were able to raise a couple million dollars in venture capital. They continued to work hard and became even more successful. They were the rave of all of the business magazines in our area. They won awards and were highly regarded. However, bit by bit, as financial challenges hit, they sought out more venture capital. But each time, they also signed away a bit more of their lives, to the point where the venture capitalists had diluted the ownership of the company they had sacrificed so much to build. Now my friend is at a point where he has minimal ownership in the company, and yet he is contractually obligated to run it for the venture capitalists. Of course, the venture capitalists demand that he put in the same amount of work and energy as when he started the company. After years of hard work, he still never gets to spend the time with his family that he was hoping this business would allow. He is now middle-aged, and he is burned out. If he would have stayed on his initial course and built his business a little more slowly, he could have zigged and zagged his way to permanent success. He now either has to start all over or continue to work in a company he no longer controls. There are times and places for venture capital, but not as frequently as people think, and it is not my desired funding method.

I Control the Finances of My Business

I have learned the hard way that every time I do not keep my finger on the pulse of the finances of my company, it goes into the weeds. Once, I returned from a vacation in Nepal to find that my partner had obligated us to a bunch of expenses without our having the income to pay for them. To cover his commitments, he basically sold off our inventory in a fire sale. He was so proud that he had sold so much product, but he did not bother to look at the bottom line, and we took a huge loss on the items he sold. He seemed to have forgotten that sales don't really count for much if they don't actually make a profit.

I really do not love doing the finances, but I have learned that no one else is going to manage my money the way I manage it. I always pay my bills on time, and I always know exactly how much is in my bank account. I simply do not spend money I do not have, and if I'm not keeping track of my finances, I know I could find myself in a position that would force me outside of my guardrails.

I WILL NOT MAKE PERSONAL GUARANTEES ON THINGS THAT I HAVE NO CONTROL OVER

Years ago, I was hired as a young CEO of a small start-up company. I did not have ownership, but I was eager to impress the owners and show that I was in the game. The company needed a batch of new computers for the employees. I thought I was demonstrating my commitment by volunteering to sign for the lease on these new computers. So, I signed a personal guarantee that obligated me to a three-year lease. Needless to say, the business collapsed along with the rest of the Internet bubble. Here I was without a job, and I had to pay $800 each month toward these computers. I brought them home and lined them up in my basement. They had absolutely no value to me, other than my kids learned great computer skills. I did fulfill my obligation, but I vowed never to sign a personal guarantee on something over which I do not have complete control.

I Protect My Personal Network

One of my guardrails is that I will protect my personal network. I've been offered countless opportunities to get involved in businesses that would have been dependent on tapping into my networks of family and close personal friends. At times, I would have been looking to them for capital. At other times, I would have been using them as my primary pool to market to. For me personally, I'm very protective of my family and friends because I know that they will be very hard to replace if a business goes south.

I Stay Focused on My Values

I try to always ensure that my business life conforms to my personal beliefs and values. Obviously, I will not do anything that is illegal or unethical. For some, that line may be a bit fuzzy, but my guardrail is whether I would ever have to justify or rationalize my actions to my wife or my children (or my mother!).

Sometimes, my decisions are made by the simple measure of whether an opportunity feels right to me. Not long ago, I was approached about doing business with an individual who was manufacturing and selling diet products. The opportunity seemed promising, so I went home and told my wife about it. Given her experience as a registered nurse, she examined the product and then told me why she felt it was not safe and why she felt this venture wasn't something I should have my name associated with. The product was perfectly legal. But it was not something my wife believed in, so I did not pursue the opportunity.

EATING OUR OWN COOKING

In our current test business, Curtis and I received a request from a client that wanted to place a large order for high-end, specialty products. We went to the manufacturer of these products and were able to open an account. However, when it came time to sign the contract with the vendor, it contained language prohibiting our operating a business model that was *identical* to *our* business model. The order we were trying to fill was worth a large sum of money. And the likelihood of the vendor ever figuring out we were in violation of the contract was minimal. In our zeal to land this account, Curtis and I conveniently forgot to pay close attention to this clause in the contract. However, Koral, who is one of my trusted gatekeepers, reminded us that signing the contract would run counter

OUT-OF-BOUNDS WORKSHEET

LIST THE PEOPLE THAT YOU TRUST TO TELL YOU WHEN YOU ARE OUT-OF-BOUNDS. THIS IS YOUR "OUT-OF-BOUNDS" NETWORK

LIST THE GUARDRAILS THAT WILL KEEP YOU FROM GOING OUT-OF-BOUNDS.

LIST 4 OR 5 WAYS YOU WILL KNOW WHEN YOU ARE HEADING OUT-OF-BOUNDS. IS IT A GUT FEELING, PANIC, SCARCITY MIND-SET OR SOMETHING ELSE?

REFER BACK TO THE RESOURCE LIST IN CHAPTER 4 TO DETERMINE EXACTLY WHERE YOU NEED TO CHANGE DIRECTION ON EACH ZIG AND ZAG. LIST THOSE DIRECTION CHANGES.

HAVE A DIRECT CONVERSATION WITH EACH MEMBER OF YOUR OUT-OF-BOUNDS NETWORK. MAKE SURE THEY CLEARLY UNDERSTAND WHAT YOUR GUARDRAILS ARE AND WHAT THEIR RESPONSIBILITY IS TO KEEP YOU WITHIN THOSE BOUNDS.

to our values. As lucrative as this deal would have been to our company, we passed on the order. It just seemed that if we were going to lose sleep, it would be better to lose it over the loss of revenue rather than the violation of our code of conduct.

In a previous business Curtis and I founded, we did not follow our own guardrails. We had put a financial guardrail in place stating that we would always keep a $100,000, three-month buffer in place to protect us if the business took a downturn. We also agreed that if things went south, we would reduce expenses, rather than dip into our reserve, in order to maintain a positive cash flow.

After several years of mind-blowing success, the business did suffer a downturn. It wasn't long before we saw ourselves dipping below the $100,000 threshold. At the time we had a team we felt loyal to, and we did not want to have to cut back. So we lowered our threshold to $50,000. In making that decision, we broke our rule and crashed through our guardrail. But we felt justified in doing so because of our previous success. Before we knew it, we had crashed through the guardrail again and spent that last $50,000. At this point, instead of cutting our losses, we decided to create another business plan. Unfortunately, our team was not a good match for our new venture. Ultimately, with no cash left, we had to lay off the entire team we had been trying to protect. We also had to terminate what had been a very productive partnership and part ways.

We would have all been so much better off if we had reduced our expenses and stayed within that first guardrail. Yes, we would have had to lay off one or two employees or cut back on expenses in some other way. As painful as that sounds, it would have been so much better than having to kill the whole business. We could have saved our most valuable employees and avoided a lot of pain and heartache.

Our blunder led to Curtis and me parting ways for almost four years. Now we are working together again and building a successful business. And we're hoping we will have the good sense not to forget our need to stay within the guardrails we've established.

Summary

As you are traveling toward your beacon in the fog, you will need guardrails to keep you from heading over a cliff or wandering out into the weeds. For each of your zigs, you should establish a financial number, an allocation of time, a duration of time, and a financial target to control the resources and energy you are going to put into that particular zig. You then need to create a list of the other guardrails that will keep you out of the weeds. Finally, remember the need to establish a network of trusted associates who will keep you from heading out of bounds or drifting toward the edge of a cliff. These guardrails will grow out of and be aligned with the values you defined in Chapter 3. They will then have the power to keep you on target as you zigzag toward your beacon in the fog.

Rewards–Finding Hidden Treasures

As you have been rushing from goal to goal or from zig to zag, have you ever found yourself asking, "Why am I doing this?" If you haven't created and implemented a system of rewards for yourself and those around you, you're going to find yourself burning out long before you reach your beacon in the fog. Success and money alone are insufficient motivators. I have found that if I tie a reward to the successful completion of each zig, I stay far more motivated than if I never pause to enjoy some benefit specifically tied to its completion. And I find I'm much more enthused about beginning the next zag.

We humans are really not much different from Pavlov's salivating dogs. If we catch a glimpse of a slab of meat, we will drool, salivate, and do just about anything to get to it. My family has what I view as a miserable little dog that is half poodle and half Chihuahua. She is the most high maintenance little mutt I have ever met. She does not like me, and I do not like her. The problem is the rest of my family loves this dog, so she and I have to put up with each other.

She will have absolutely nothing to do with me, unless I have a little piece of meat in my hand. Then she views me as her best friend, and her behavior shifts dramatically. She pants and begs and pleads for that little piece of meat. And, more important, she will do anything I ask. Interestingly, she does not like just any kind of meat. She likes the little slices of cheap lunchmeat that I am sure are not healthy for dogs. Our other dog will eat anything I give her, but not this little mutt. From the day we got her, I have had to find the things that specifically work for her.

We all have things that motivate us. The legendary football coach Vince Lombardi is attributed with saying, "Coaches who can outline plays on a blackboard are a dime a dozen. The ones who win get inside their player and motivate."

Recognizing that reality, and then consciously and deliberately motivating yourself and your teams using rewards, is one of the most powerful tools I have found, whether it's in my personal, family, or professional life.

When planning and executing each zig and zag, you should attach a reward to each target. If you find the right rewards for your people, once they hit their goal they will be willing and even anxious to turn toward the next goal.

Every great leader knows how to motivate people. It does not matter if you are a CEO, a coach, a schoolteacher, a middle manager, or a parent: a big part of your job is being the psychologist or therapist who knows how to put out little rewards that get the people around you to behave consistently in working toward the goals you've established. Lee Iacocca said, "Start with good people, lay out the rules, communicate with your employees, motivate them, and reward them. If you do all of those things effectively, you can't miss" (Lee Iococca [b. 1924]. U.S. Businessman. *Talking Straight,* Chapter 4, "Good Business—More in Management," 1988).

WHAT WILL MOTIVATE YOUR PEOPLE?

Before developing your system of rewards, remember that what motivates one person may not motivate the next. When I was general manager of About.com's web services division, I had working for me a highly talented engineer named Earl. He was, without question, one of our brightest engineers, but

I continually struggled to figure out how to motivate this guy. I regularly gave out bonuses, rewards, and incentives that everyone else loved but Earl did not seem to care about. Nothing I offered seemed to motivate him, and I knew his contributions were affected by his apathy toward my rewards system.

As we were planning our first Christmas party, I finally figured out what motivated Earl. During a planning session, he asked if he could play a piano number for the entertainment. I didn't think much about it, but told him that would be fine. The night of the Christmas party, Earl walked in, all decked out in a tuxedo, complete with flowing tails. When he sat down to play the piano, it was clear he cared deeply about his performance, and he delivered his delightful number with the flair of a concert pianist. Everyone cheered and clapped for him, and then he stood up and gave an overly exaggerated bow. From that point forward, I knew what motivated him. He didn't care about things or money. He loved recognition and any opportunity to perform and take a bow.

As the New Year began, I implemented what I dubbed "Lunch and Learn with Earl." Twice each month, we'd have a Lunch and Learn where the company would buy lunch and the junior engineers could visit with this master engineer. They would ask him questions, he would impart his wisdom, and at the end they would all clap and Earl would beam. The junior engineers learned a great deal from Earl, and Earl loved the recognition. Productivity went through the roof.

I had another employee who would always get really excited about the rewards I proposed, but before she achieved her goal, she would simply go out and buy the same thing she was going to be rewarded with. And while she did good work, I knew she could be doing far more. This pattern caused me immense frustration, but I finally found out that what she really wanted was for us to pay for her tuition at school and call it a scholarship. By listening carefully to things she said, I learned that her parents had plenty of money, but they had always drilled into their children how they had gone through college on scholarships. This young woman had good grades, but because she had no real financial need, she hadn't been able to get a scholarship. So, I developed a reward system that provided her with the scholarship she so desperately wanted.

It's also important to figure out what the people you are trying to motivate *do not* want. I've learned that a reward for one person may actually feel like a punishment for another. A few years ago, we established a reward for the young men who were working for CastleWave to go to Las Vegas and see the Blue Man Group. We set up a very specific goal and also very specific rewards, which included going to the Stratosphere and riding on a roller coaster set atop of one of the tallest hotels that juts out over the city. These boys, with one exception, worked extra hard because they loved the idea of this trip. When they weren't focused on the work, it was all they talked about. The exception happened to be a different personality type. He was one of our key engineers who was a little shy and did not like big crowds. In fact, the thought of going to Las Vegas with a bunch of loud teenagers couldn't have been less motivating.

Gratefully, he came to me and let me know that he really did not want to go on this trip. So, I found something else that motivated this engineer, and took the other boys when they reached their goal. If I had ignored his needs, the outcome might have been tragic. He was a key member of the team, and he could have subconsciously tried to sabotage the goal for the rest of the group because he did not want to go on the trip.

KEEP YOUR SYSTEM SIMPLE

It's important not to overcomplicate your system of goals and rewards. In one of my early ventures, I created a chart that had 18 different targets to hit and a simple "REWARD" written across the top. My employees were unclear as to what the priorities were and what the reward would be. Since then, I have found it's best to have three or four target goals to hit, with a very specific reward at the end. The goals we typically fail to achieve are the ones that are complex and unclear.

Employees should also feel free to devise their own systems (within reason, of course). My son and his friends came up with their own motivating reward. They had a Burger King crown they kept in the office. They were all highly competitive, and they would have contests to see which one could create the most web links on a given day. The winner then got to wear the crown. The reward didn't cost me anything, and it was fun to see these 17-year-old boys engage in an all-out push to optimize their websites just for the reward of wearing a paper crown.

One of the benefits of having a team set its own goals and rewards is that the members learn to govern their own behavior. That way I don't have to micromanage my teams.

AVOID THE ENTITLEMENT MENTALITY

When I was managing Mitsubishi Electric, I was still young and not completely financially stable personally. I had an awesome killer team that was also young and hungry. I began the practice of taking them out to lunch every Friday. I would pay for their lunch myself because I didn't feel the company should have that expense. This was my personal way of showing my appreciation. A few months into this, I ended up in a tough stretch where I was traveling almost nonstop. As a result, there were a few Fridays where we didn't make it to lunch. Soon, there was muttering and complaining. Morale dropped. These employees had become so accustomed to going to lunch each Friday that they felt they were entitled to this perk. What started as a good intention led to my being the bad guy because I did not consistently provide them with their expected lunch.

I had a similar experience with my crew of teenagers. I would stock the fridge with food and soda pops so they could grab something to eat after they finished school and before they started to work. A few times we got so busy I failed to replenish the quickly consumed food items. Almost immediately, some of the boys started murmuring, "I can't believe it, there aren't any burritos or Hot Pockets in the fridge." If I have erred, it is because sometimes I have rewarded too quickly or too often.

ALLOW FOR SOME FLEXIBILITY

Situations change, and sometimes you need to change with them. I've lived through shifts in markets where even though my team gave an incredible effort, they fell a bit short of the original goal. In those situations I still gave the reward so the team didn't lose steam. However, be careful not to reward when the reward is not merited.

I employ a group of mothers who work for me from their homes. They are motivated and hardworking. I told them once that if they accomplished 10 consecutive days of making $500 in profit per day, I would give each of them a large bonus. These women worked their hearts out. At the end of the period, I saw that while they were only clearing $300 to $400 on the weekdays, on the weekend their profits were $800 to $1,000. Even though they did not achieve the 10 consecutive days of $500 a day, on an average they were well over the target I had set. I told them that in this instance, average really does count for something, and they earned their reward.

The Whip

I've had partners who used the whip. There certainly are times when you have to discipline. However, my contention is that the whip needs to be used very sparingly—and never as an immediate reaction. If you whip someone (verbally, of course), you may get a burst of incredible performance. But you will inevitably lose your long-term productivity (and your top performers) if you punish too often.

I have seen people who use the whip over and over. Soon the people around them reach the breaking point and basically say, "I don't care. Whip me to death. I am done." They check out, and apathy sets in. I know a young, up-and-coming executive who was a master with the whip. Unfortunately, he was so hungry to prove himself that he burned through all the people around him. Now, no one in our area will work for him.

There is a fine balance between knowing when to reward and knowing when to discipline. When there is an out-of-bounds problem, discipline needs to be meted out. In our home, we do not have the long lists of rules I have seen some parents enforce. Instead, the rules we do have are rules that fit with our core values, and we are very strict with these few rules. I often say to my kids. "You will make some mistakes. That is how you learn. Just don't make the *big* mistakes!" Too many little rules can create confusion and can actually undermine the more important rules.

SEEING THE VALUE IN FAILURE

In my current company, we have created four sets of quarterly goals for this year. Honestly, I hope we miss one of these goals. I do not want to miss the first set or the second, but if we miss the third set of goals, it gives me an opportunity to point out that this is what a little failure feels like and your success is not guaranteed. I've managed teams that developed a bit too much ego. That can lead to arrogance and missed goals. If you handle such situations well, it will bring your team back to where they're hungry and want to win again.

DON'T GIVE OUT REWARDS UNTIL THEY ARE ACTUALLY EARNED

Being a fundamentally nice guy, I have made the mistake multiple times of giving a reward when the performance didn't warrant it. Every time that I have done this, I have ended up regretting it. Even though you may feel for a minute that you've done the right thing, you've likely created a pattern and behavior system that will bite you in the end. In some cases, being "nice" has been the death knell of my businesses.

My family and I have traveled to Nepal several times, and I am always overwhelmed by the rampant poverty. Like anyone who has traveled there, I have been approached countless times by small children who must beg in the streets for what little they have, and I always ponder what I—as one person with limited means—can do to help.

The last time we were there, several young beggars followed my sons, our two Sherpas, and me everywhere we went. They were filthy, and their ragged clothes were soaked with urine. They approached us repeatedly, gesturing to their mouths and then their stomachs to show us they were hungry.

I believe that giving a person a handout does little to change his or her circumstances, but it broke my heart to see these small boys, who were about the ages of my younger boys. Then I hit upon an idea.

We were in the middle of a central square where countless people gather each day to worship and shop. While there are numerous trash cans in the square, no one seems to use them, and the area is covered with what looks like years of debris. I decided I could solve two problems at once, so I offered one of the beggars 100 rupees (about $1.40) for every bag of trash he picked up and put in a trash can. Given that the daily income for an adult in Nepal is about $2, that seemed like a powerful incentive.

What I was asking would have taken a couple of minutes, but this little boy looked at me like I was nuts and ran off. Another little boy approached me, and I made the same offer. He indicated he would do it, but wanted payment up front. Now, I may be a soft touch, but I'm not stupid, so I told him he would get paid upon completion of the work. He, too, ran off.

The third boy who approached me was the dirtiest and scrawniest of the bunch. I really thought my plan had merit, so I upped the offer to 500 rupees. His initial reaction was to give me a look that said, "No one picks up trash. Not even beggars. What kind of crazy American are you?" But this time, I grabbed a bag and started picking up trash myself. He soon joined in and was stuffing trash into his bag as quickly as he could. There was so much trash that our efforts were like trying to drain a pond using a teaspoon, but we were at least doing something to make a dent. And soon others were joining in, including a gentleman who runs a humanitarian organization who saw my impetuous project as having some potential.

When we finished working and I paid the boy, he couldn't have been more proud. And several shopkeepers around the square began making similar offers to other boys who clearly were in need.

I realize that we made a very small dent in the problems of world hunger and cleaning up the environment that day. But I also know that those who watched, including my sons, learned that rewards need to be based on our efforts, not our wishes—and that the right reward system can provide the motivation to get to work and make a difference.

Reward Yourself

Some people are good about rewarding team members and employees, but they're not so good at rewarding themselves. I've fallen into that trap myself more than once; but I think I've finally learned that if I have an emotional meltdown, it's usually because I haven't followed through on feeding my inner self.

Just as I was taking the frightening leap from being employed at a full-time job to being a full-time entrepreneur, I was playing basketball and blew out my Achilles tendon, which had to be repaired surgically. Six weeks later, while pushing too hard at my physical therapy, I blew it out again. This was a tough time. It's not in my nature to sit around, but all I could do was sit in my bed and work on my computer. I had started a small business, but there was very little I could do to move it forward. I knew that I had the choice to either sink or swim, but I felt myself sinking—and fast.

I finally called my partners into my bedroom, where we talked about our predicament. In mapping out what we could do to salvage the situation, I proposed that if we achieved the success we had our sights on, we would reward ourselves, together with our wives, by going on a cruise. We went to work, and as I lay in bed day after day, I pictured success as sitting with my partners and our wives on an upper deck, toasting our success as we watched the sun set. That image drove me to achieve my goals, even though the odds were stacked against me.

We did indeed hit our goal, and I cannot convey the depth of my joy and satisfaction as we sat around that table and I offered this simple toast, "We did it. We made it."

With that lesson in mind, consider what would have happened had we not taken the celebratory trip? All too often, people intend to give themselves rewards, but then they become martyrs. They start thinking, "I am just too busy," or "I should put this money back into the business." I know that had I not taken that dreamed-about cruise, my subconscious would have revolted, which would have damaged my desire to dig deep and sacrifice in the future.

I use little rewards throughout the day to motivate myself, particularly when I'm really having a tough day. When I'm dealing with difficult issues, I might tell myself something like, "When I get through this, I'm going to go outside and smell the air, and I'm going to watch the ducks for 10 minutes." There are all kinds of ways we can reward ourselves quietly throughout the day, and they can help us keep our head above water.

EATING OUR OWN COOKING

Last year my wife and I went on a little getaway to Las Vegas. We had booked our hotel online, and we got a great rate on a normal room at one of the nicest hotels in Vegas. When we checked in, the woman at the front desk took a liking to us. She saw that we were on a romantic getaway, and she mentioned that most of the regular rooms were booked for a business convention. As she handed us our key cards, she mentioned she had upgraded our room, adding, "I am not going to tell you about the room now. You can thank me later when you see it."

When we opened the door to our room, we gasped. She had upgraded our $69 room to one of the presidential suites.

It was on the twenty-seventh floor and had a 180-degree view of Las Vegas. The suite was 2,200 square feet. It came with an entryway, a formal dining area, a living area, a huge bedroom, and two bathrooms. My favorite part was the master bath suite. It had an all-glass shower and a huge hot tub that overlooked the city. And we did, indeed, thank this very kind front-end manager.

When I came back after this spectacular vacation with my wife, I was describing to Curtis this hotel we stayed in. At this point in our business, Curtis was still working full time in his other job, and we were not making the progress we wanted in this new partnership. As we chatted, it hit me that I knew what would motivate Curtis. He wanted to take his wife on a vacation and stay at the same hotel my wife and I had just enjoyed—and in the same room!

I told him I had a reward in mind, and we made a list of four or five things that needed to happen. We posted this list in the hall of our office, along with a picture of this fantastic resort. The goal was that when those five steps were achieved and our business was stabilized, Curtis could quit his job and come into the business full time. But equally rewarding to him was that he could also take his wife on an all-expense-paid trip to stay in this same hotel. I found a picture of this hotel and drew stick figures of Curtis and his wife staying on the twenty-seventh floor and enjoying the view. I even added a picture of its world-renowned restaurant because I knew his wife likes to dine at exclusive restaurants. On the bottom of my artwork, I added a deadline of 35 days to earn this reward.

Curtis was salivating, even though we were not sure how this was going to happen. But we did reach each of our goals, and Curtis and his wife did get to have a fantastic vacation. And my reward was that I now had him working with me in our business full time.

SUMMARY

When you are planning out rewards, you need to very specifically tie each reward to the zig or the zag you are heading toward. I always establish time frames, often in the form of quarterly goals. When we make our quarterly goals, we sit down as a team and decide what we want to accomplish. Once we have established the goal, we spend almost as much time discussing what reward we will get when we achieve the goal.

Then we make signs and post them all over the office, with the goal written out above a picture of the reward.

One of the signs I used in our office had a picture of people snowmobiling. We titled it, "Plowing Our Way to Victory." Around the picture were listed the goals of getting three new clients and having a financial target of monthly recurring profit. Another goal was to hire one more engineer and to retain another engineering client.

For the business my son and his friends work on, they helped me develop a very specific reward for hitting certain targets. They then posted pictures of the cruise ship we would all board if they met their goals and also the ports we would visit. Sure enough, each of them achieved the goals, and we went for a one-week cruise.

As you set long-term goals, don't overlook the need to reward yourself and your team along the way. These in-between rewards are ones I like to keep random. Then, when I see a team member doing a particularly good job at something, I will hand that member a pair of movie tickets or a gift card. The other day, we sent one of our contract employees a special "thank you" that he was not expecting. Ever since then, he has gone over and above on the work that he does for us because that little reward meant so much to him. Sometimes, random rewards will actually mean more than guaranteeing a treat when you push the same button over and over.

The work you're doing is challenging and difficult, and as you hit each zig, you need to take a break from the intensity, celebrate, and enjoy the fruits of your labors. Then you can do a little jump and turn your skis in the other direction toward the next goal. We humans do have some things in common with my little, salivating dog. When we align our efforts with little treats along the way, our resulting behaviors will lead to achieving our goals. The rewards make all of the effort worthwhile.

Avoiding the All-or-Nothing Trap

I grew up in a rural community. My father was completely blind. I am the oldest of four sons, and as long as I can remember I have had entrepreneurial desires. Despite some lofty ambitions, I was never any kind of a stand-out kid. I was one of those boys who was often overlooked, and I spent a lot of time hoping I wasn't the last kid picked on the basketball team. Nonetheless, I had this incredible and deep desire to do something of significance with my life.

I remember when I was 18 years old and just finishing up high school; I wrote down some personal goals. I had always been goal-oriented, and my mother encouraged me to write down my goals. One of those goals was to become the CEO of a major company. Even though I wrote it down, I knew it was as far off of a goal as I could have set. I didn't think there was any chance in the world of actually ever reaching that goal; in fact, I might as well have written that I was going to sprout wings and flap my way to the moon. And yet that became a powerful goal. It was my beacon in the fog.

I was very fortunate to have been able to get a good education. After graduating, I worked hard and had some incredible opportunities. And I ended up having the opportunity to work as a CEO and a general manager at some large and well-known companies. Midway through my career in corporate America, I was given a leadership role in a large, international organization. I was eager and determined to earn my stripes, and I basically committed to do so at all costs. I was a very young general manager of the U.S. division, and I was determined to do anything that was necessary to succeed. My commitment bordered on insane. I had a young family, but I was traveling hundreds of thousands of miles every year. There were nights I would stay at the office all night long to do what I felt needed to be done. I was going to succeed, and I didn't care about the costs.

Then I learned the lesson that it is not worth risking everything of importance in your life to achieve success.

The division I headed became very successful. In the middle of our run, my mentor and boss, Dr. Peter Horne, called my secretary and said, "I need to have a visit with Rich." That meant jumping on a plane, flying to Atlanta, then from Atlanta to Amsterdam, and from Amsterdam across the channel to Birmingham, England. Door-to-door, this was a 22-hour trip.

When I arrived, Dr. Horne pulled me into his office and sat me down. He then said, "Rich, we're really delighted with the progress you've made in the business. Things are coming along rather nicely." And then he made this comment, which has stuck with me: "I want you to remember one thing, Rich. You can replace almost anything in this world. You can replace a car. You can replace a job. You can replace money. But you can't replace your health, you can't replace your trust relationships, and, most important, you can't replace your family." Then he shooed me out of his office, and I began the long journey home.

Those 20 hours, which I spent alone on a very crowded airplane, gave me plenty of time to think about what Dr. Horne had just said. Most of my thoughts centered on my wife and children. For years I had been telling my wife, "This next project is a big one for me. I am going to give it my all for six months, so don't plan on seeing much of me. But once I finish it, things will be different." The six months would pass. I would complete the project, and then a new project would come along and I would start the cycle all over again. Those six months had turned into years as I kept promising, "If I give my all to this for six months, then we will have it made."

As I flew back across the Alantic, I reflected on a trip I had taken to India some months before. When I got home, all of my sons and I came down with whooping cough, or pertussis. We had all been immunized, but somehow we contracted this miserable illness. It was terrible. I remember coughing so hard that I would frequently vomit, but I lacked the discipline to take time off from my work to get better and help my wife with our sons. My youngest son at the time was Nathan. He was less than a year old when we all got sick, and it was life-threatening for him. In fact, he ended up in the hospital, where my wife took care of him because I was too busy.

Flying home, I realized I was falling into the "all-or-nothing trap," and I resolved that I was going to do better as a father and husband. The first thing I did when I got home was to gather my young sons together, give them each a hug, and tell them I love them. But when I went to pick up Nathan, he hollered and screamed. As he pushed me away, I realized he did not even know who I was. At that moment, I realized that achieving my goal of being a CEO was not worth losing the love of my family. And I began to change both my priorities and how I actually lived my life.

Now, that doesn't mean I lost my intensity. It doesn't mean that I never end up out of balance. But my short session with Dr. Horne brought great clarity to the fact that it's not worth giving up the things that matter most for the things that matter least. This insight was part of what helped me see the Zigzag

Principle as a far better way to approach life. Now, as I zig and zag from goal to goal, I will still put intense effort into achieving my dreams. But at each turn, I've established a reward that for me inevitably includes my family (your rewards, of course, may differ). And for each goal I pursue, I set up guardrails that will determine the amount of time and effort I am willing to invest. There are not many ways to succeed without going out of balance for a period of time. The key is to realize that you *are* going out of balance for a short period and then bounce back and take some time off to enjoy your life.

My philosophy involves a line of balance. Many people think you achieve balance by being at work exactly at 8 a.m. and leaving within minutes of 5 p.m., by getting eight hours of sleep each night, and by controlling life with a rigid schedule. I don't live my life that way. At times I live my life extremely out of balance. I'll work so crazy hard that I think I'm going to die, and then I'll cross over and go for a cruise where I sleep 18 hours a day. Then I'll charge back across the line and spend some incredible family time, then I'll go work my guts out again and not sleep for a couple or three weeks while I start another new business. Then I'll spend a month in the Himalayas with my family. The way I define balance is not to try walking the perfect line, but to cross that line of balance as frequently as possible. This is the final form of zigzagging I would suggest.

Added to my own bad example of having spent my early years charging straight toward my goals is the example of an individual who completed his MBA program the same time

I did. He was a charismatic and brilliant man. He had every-thing going for him—far more than the rest of us did, really. During school and after we graduated, he was fixated on the same path I was on. He was going to the top, and he was going to succeed at all costs. I guess the only real difference between us is that I am fortunate enough to have a wife who has helped me become grounded and remember what really matters in my life. (Sometimes she has had to beat me over the head to make her point, but I count that as a form of help.)

This man was relentless in his pursuit of wealth. He racked up frequent-flier miles and spent even more time away from his family than I did. He did whatever it took to get to the top, and he got there. In fact, by traditional measures, he has achieved a level of success I might have been envious of at one point in my life. But now, as I look back over my life and this man's life, I see some significant differences. He has been married and divorced multiple times. He has had more flings than I can count with my hands and my toes. He has no relationship with his children; in fact, they will not even talk to him.

I look at him, and I am so grateful that Dr. Horne took the time to counsel with me—and then put me on a transatlantic flight to think about what he said. As a result, my son Nathan, who would not let me touch him because he did not know who I was, now calls me his hero. Success is not worth heading over a cliff or getting so out of balance that we lose control. Everything in life requires balance. The best skiers cross that line of balance as often as possible as they race down the hill.

But they know how to keep their momentum and stay upright through the race, rather than crashing and burning.

A key to maintaining our balance in life and in business is not getting so tightly wound up and so intense that we do not get in a rhythm, or what the best athletes call "flow." In his book, *Golf Is Not a Game of Perfect,* sports psychologist Bob Rotella, who has worked with many of the world's greatest golfers, talks about the mind-set that the best golfers have to get into. When golfers are playing at their peak, Rotella says, they are only using a part of their brain while the other part is shut down. It is almost as if they are in a trance. Things just come naturally to them. They are relaxed, and they let the intuitive and creative part of their brain do the work. That is flow.

Many of us, on the other hand, get so stressed and uptight that we create our own failures. Our stress then creates a form of reverse psychology, similar to what happens when I'm golfing and see a water hazard off to the left. If I allow myself to think (which Rotella would suggest I *not* do!), I tell myself, "Don't go left into the water." And, just like that, the ball invariably ends up going dead left into the pond. The same thing is true as we pursue our beacons in the fog. If we get fixated on the things we think we can't do or if we get consumed with the possibility of a little error or failure, we get wound up too tight. And that actually translates into negative behaviors that undercut our efforts.

I experienced this phenomenon recently in our business with a client who is one of our biggest and longest-standing customers. Where he was once a pleasure to work with, he had

185

become more difficult, demanding, and disrespectful. He felt our terms and conditions didn't apply to him. Because we felt such a need to hang on to him, we would make accommodations, which led us to breaking our own rules, abandoning our processes, and crashing through our guardrails. In short, we didn't want to lose him, and we held on too tightly.

Finally, Curtis and I got pushed to the point where we realized we had wasted far too much energy on this client—and that we were holding on too tight. So, we began to let go a little bit. We knew we might lose his business, but we decided that was better than the alternative. Rather than chasing after him in a desperate mind-set, we adopted a "take it or leave it" attitude, believing that if things didn't work out with this customer, we would find another one. And that keeps us out of the "all-or-nothing" trap.

In the end, the Zigzag Principle will help us avoid the "all-or-nothing trap" as we work our way toward our beacons in the fog, whereas a straight line will lead us straight into the weeds. I once listened to Jeff Sandefer, a university professor and Harvard MBA who *Bloomberg Businessweek* named one of the top entrepreneurship professors in the United States. Jeff spoke of a final exam he gave his MBA students, who were required to speak with 10 seasoned and successful executives. Jeff further specified that the first three executives they interviewed needed to be highly successful, but under the age of 35. The next three successful executives were to be in their mid-forties and fifties. The final four interviews were to be with successful executives who were in the final stages of their careers.

In each of the interviews, Jeff's students were to elicit information on how these executives pursued and viewed success.

Invariably, the young bucks were beating their chests and chasing after the brass ring, often in ways that put them at risk of losing their balance. The middle-aged executives were beginning to figure life out. Some of them had regrets and others had chosen to add some balance to their lives.

Of course, it was the older executives who gave the real insight. It did not matter what type of business these men or women were involved with. In each case, they described a pattern of pursuing success that was guided by these three questions:

1. Was it honorable?
2. Did it leave an impact?
3. Who loves me and who do I love?

Many of these older executives were billionaires. And yet they talked very little about money. What mattered to them was how their business helped others and whether their business mattered. They wanted to leave a legacy. And most important, they talked about the people who loved them and the people they loved. Of course, there were those who did not have loved ones, and they talked about that absence with regret. They were honest and open and direct about their successes and their mistakes.

Whatever our goals are, whatever our beacon in the fog is, it is critical that we do what we do for the proper reasons and that we stay within the guardrails and values that we have set for ourselves. If we do, we will get to the end of our lives— a day which will inevitably come—and have no regrets.

The Zigzag Principle is a disciplined approach to business and life. It is not an "easy" approach; in fact, it requires incredible effort to traverse the mountain before you as you make your way to your destination. But being willing to zigzag—and then doing it with control—will help you build a business and a life that will be stable and strong.

As we wrap up this journey we've taken together, I want to reiterate the underpinnings of the Zigzag Principle:

You must begin by creating a foundation.

⇨ First, you need to look deep into you pockets and see what resources you have right now.

⇨ Second, you must determine what your beacon in the fog is going to be.

⇨ Third, you must identify and hold to the values you are going to follow in pursuit of that particular goal.

⇨ And, finally, you must fuel your efforts with passion and determination.

Once your foundation is set, you can begin to zig and zag toward your goal.

⇨ The first zig is always to get to profitability. If you do not meet this goal, then you must try something different and keep trying until you get your business or your life profitable.

⇨ The second zag is to use the cash from the previous zig to add resources. This requires you to let go just a bit and teach other people how to travel with you in pursuit of your dream.

⇨ The third zig is to scale your business. This is the part when you are working *on* your business, not *in* your business.

There will be more zigs and zags as you work toward your final beacon in the fog.

⇨ Look forward and plan three zigs ahead. The third zig out can be adjusted and changed to match the terrain of the trail you are following.

⇨ Your zigs and zags need to be bound by guardrails. These guardrails are the things that will keep you away from the trees, the weeds, and the cliffs. They are always aligned with your values.

⇨ Each zig and zag is bound by how much money, time, and personal resources you have predetermined to put toward your goal.

⇨ In each case, there is a financial target you need to achieve before you can turn toward the next zig, and this target is always bound by your knowing what you can and can't afford to lose.

As you hit each zig, there will be a planned reward.

⇨ The rewards are the motivation that will make you and those around you choose to make that turn toward your next zag.

I set some very ambitious goals for myself when I was a rather ordinary young man living in rural Utah. At the time, I was determined to achieve success in life, and I considered a straight line to be the path to follow in achieving those goals. When I mowed lawns to save for college, I loved to finish a job and look back at those straight lines I had created. If there was a door in my way, I didn't see any need to open it to get to the other side. If there was a cinderblock wall between me and my goal, I was generally smart enough to recognize my need to go around it, but not without considerable resentment and a consideration of the odds of my crashing straight through.

Given all of the skiing and mountain climbing I've done, coupled with my wife's insistence that we not chart our course to Disneyland as the crow flies, it's curious to me that it took me as long as it did to realize that zigzagging really is both a law of nature *and* (with few exceptions) the most effective way of getting to where we're headed. But I finally did come to that realization, and by adopting a philosophy that was once antithetical to my very nature, I have achieved considerably more success, even as I have maintained my sanity and my sense of balance and control over those things in my life that matter most.

While this book has, at times, focused on business settings and practices, the Zigzag Principle can be used in any part of your life. It changes the rules from "one strike and you're out" or "it's all or nothing" to principles that help you navigate toward your beacon in the fog.

You may miss the mark sometimes. That's fine, as long as you take a minute to get your head above the fog and pinpoint once again where you're headed. And as long as your zigs and zags are guided by your catalyzing statements.

There is nothing more satisfying to me than standing with a son at the bottom of a ski slope and examining the tracks we've made in getting down a seemingly impossible slope. Or standing on a jagged mountain summit with my wife and children and retracing our steps to the top. Both are remarkable views—ones that I hope you too will enjoy.

Index

About the Author

Rich Christiansen describes himself as "a perfectly good business executive, turned entrepreneur."

Before becoming an entrepreneur, he was a skilled executive and market innovator in the corporate world. He was general manager at both Mitsubishi Electric and About.com. After 20 years in the technology industry, he discovered that his true passion and talent is in launching start-up companies.

Rich has founded or cofounded 32 businesses, which were bootstrapped with just $5,000 to $10,000 of starting capital. Eleven of those endeavors were miserable failures, but 11 have become wildly successful multimillion-dollar businesses. Rich has identified the Zigzag Principle as his secret formula for optimizing success while minimizing failure. It is also his methodology for setting goals and living a happy, healthy life.

Using this principle, Rich is having a blast building, managing, and selling his own compilation of start-up companies. He states, "I am not sure it should be legal for one individual to have this much fun."

The Zigzag Principle is a part of every facet of Rich's life—including his personal, professional, and family life. He even teaches and empowers his own children to apply the principles to build their own successful businesses.

When the family is not starting a new venture, the Christiansens enjoy cruises, traveling the world, and spending time outdoors. They recently returned from Nepal after trekking in the Himalayas together. Rich is committed to his beautiful wife, five wonderful sons, and Nepalese daughter. They live in the spectacular mountains of Utah.

Rich received both his bachelor's degree in electronic engineering technology and his master's degree in business administration from Brigham Young University. He is passionate about educating youth in third-world countries. He has set the personal goal to help educate 1,000 young men and women before he turns 50.

Contact Rich at:
www.zigzagprinciple.com
855-ZigZag2 (855-944-9242)
info@zigzagprinciple.com